Mary: Yesterday, To

Mary

Yesterday, Today, Tomorrow

Edward Schillebeeckx and Catharina Halkes

Crossroad • New York

1993
The Crossroad Publishing Company
370 Lexington Avenue, New York, NY 10017

Translated by John Bowden from *Maria: Gisteren,
Vandaag, Morgen*, published 1992 by Uitgeverij H.
Nelissen, Baarn.

Library of Congress Cataloging-in-Publication Data

Schillebeeckx. Edward, 1941–
[Maria, English]
Mary: yesterday, today, tomorrow/Edward
Schillebeeckx and Catharina Halkes.
p.   cm.
Translation of: Maria.
Translation by John Bowden.
Includes bibliographical references.
ISBN 0–8245–1371–1
1. Mary, Blessed Virgin, Saint—History of doctrines—
20th century   I. Halkes, Catharina J. M.   II. Title
BT610.S3413   1993
232.91—dc20
93–19852
CIP

Printed in Great Britain

Contents

Foreword

A good deal has happened in recent decades in connection with Mary, both in belief and in theology. Critics increasingly ask whether her place in the Catholic church can be taken for granted: the one-sided picture of the humble, chaste mother is contrasted with quite different pictures, which are used to criticize it.

The questions and criticisms are connected with new insights into and views of the church which have developed since the Second Vatican Council.

The two authors of this book experienced the beginning of all these changes and they both – each in their own way – have become known for their theological commitment in church and society.

By looking back on their own publications from this time, they show here where the questions about Mary came from in the 1960s and what this means for thought about Mary.

Then they go into today's questions and give their own views.

In 1990, at a symposium on Mary for fellow religious, Edward Schillebeckx gave a lecture which was received enthusiastically.

The reception prompted the idea of publishing it in an appropriate form.

After much interest in the past, for some time now little has been written on Mary by theologians. Feminist theologians in particular have been responsible for reopening discussions. So Catharina

Halkes was asked to write an article to go with the one by Edward Schillebeeckx.

Together, these two articles form an interesting contribution to the development of mariology, theological thought about Mary.

This book was published on the initiative of the Edward Schillebeeckx Foundation. The aim of this Foundation is to present the theology of Edward Schillebeeckx in a way that makes it accessible to a wider public. It does not seek to isolate Schillebeeckx's work, but to offer it for discussion. So Catharina Halkes' contribution is important for avoiding a one-sided picture of Mary and showing the distinctive features of these two theologians.

This book is written by Catholic theologians, but is intended for anyone who is in search of, or fascinated by, the significance of Mary in the past and the present. The contributions invite not only study and discussion, but also personal reflection.

Marianne Merkx
Study Secretary, Edward Schillebeeckx Foundation

Introduction

Marianne Merkx

Whole libraries have been written about Mary down the centuries, in the form of sermons, theological writings, devotional literature, historical or literary works. After a short period of noticeable silence, in recent years a large quantity of works, large and small, have again appeared, including this one.

It will be clear that this is not a total study of Mary. Here we have the remarks of two theologians for whom Mary was already an important subject in the past. They show how their thought has changed and what Mary means for them today.

From Mary and the various images which are formed of her, we can see how important it is to keep approaching the tradition critically and to translate it for the situation of today. Complete abandonment of old images brings the danger of throwing the baby away with the bath water: for the generation which grew up after the Second Vatican Council, Mary is really an unknown. The old image had disappeared, and there was little to replace it. However, to hold on to existing pictures leads to alienation and produces misunderstandings. Many people, above all women, have suffered under the old image of the virgin and the mother. Fortunately this image has been shattered, but with the result that for them too Mary has come to stand at a distance. A 'new' Mary can emerge through a dialogue between past and present.

In this introduction I aim to shed some light on the articles by Catharina Halkes and Edward Schillebeeckx and put them in context, in order to clarify the significance of this material.

Although the two articles are independent, they fit well together.

I

They relate to a comparable period: both Schillebeeckx and Halkes go into their publications on Mary which appeared around the time of the Second Vatican Council and draw lines from them to present-day discussions. In this way it becomes clear how thought about Mary has changed.

The Second Vatican Council played an important role in the theological development of both Schillebeeckx and Halkes, and they were both involved in the developments after the Council in the Netherlands. Both authors indicate that their view of Mary has been changed by their theological insights, but that Mary continues to have an important place in their faith. Scripture plays a great role in their quests for Mary.

In terms of content there are also points of contact, like the criticism of the significance of Mary as 'mother' and 'virgin' and her role in redemption.

However, alongside these agreements there are clear differences, which have to do with differences in theological views and background. The most striking difference is the framework within which they develop the theme. For Schillebeeckx that is the Second Vatican Council: for Halkes it has become feminist theology. Although the frameworks are different, however, they do make contact.

In order to gain a picture of their theological positions, I shall present the views of the authors in terms of these frameworks.

Then I shall offer a brief survey of the most important developments in recent decades in connection with Mary.

I The Second Vatican Council

In retrospect, the Second Vatican Council was a starting point for a new period in the life of the Catholic church: since then, events or views have been divided into pre-Vatican II and post-Vatican II. Of course there has not been a total change in thought, but in the years of the council insights and views were developed which have become determinative for theology and the church.

Pope John XXIII announced the council in 1959; it started four years later, in October 1962, and was concluded in December 1965 with sixteen council documents. Meanwhile another pope had been elected, Paul VI. The purpose of the council was an inner reform and revival of Roman Catholic church life which at the same time would be the preparation for a later coming together of the various Christian churches. This was an ecumenical council, but in the literal meaning of the word, i.e. it was 'universal', an ecclesial assembly for the whole Roman Catholic church.[1]

Central points of this ecclesial asssembly were the shared responsibility of all believers for the church, for better or for worse,[2] and concern for society, the world. The question of believing in a world in which faith is becoming less and less a matter of course was the basic theme of the council.[3]

Although these views were shared by the majority, other notions also played a role, both during the council and afterwards. Moreover the conciliar texts have been interpreted in different ways.[4]

These years were very important for Schillebeeckx, but in turn Schillebeeckx was very important for the council and for its effects in the Netherlands. His theology cannot be understood without this council, just as conversely the church's reception of the council cannot pass over his theology.[5]

Schillebeeckx was very soon involved in the preparations for the Second Vatican Council by the Dutch bishops. Since 1958 he had been professor of dogmatics and the history of theology in the theological faculty of the Catholic University in Nijmegen. Before that he taught in the Dominican house of study in Louvain, after he had studied philosophy and theology in Louvain and gained his doctorate in theology in Paris.

He was not an 'official expert' at the council, and so was not present at the sessions. But his role as a theological adviser made him widely known. His task consisted in giving lectures to groups of bishops on the themes of the council. Schillebeeckx indicated what he thought good or bad about the proposals for the council documents from a theological perspective.[6] In addition, at the request of the Dutch bishops he wrote about modern theology and

3

produced a commentary on a preparatory scheme. The two writings had a noticeable influence on the council.[7] Back in the Netherlands Schillebeeckx sought to communicate the significance of the council through many lectures and publications and to translate the visions of renewal for the Dutch situation.

Schillebeeckx described the council like this: 'The fundamental experience of the Second Vatican Council is not so much that the Church has to be adapted to the modern era, but rather that the real and lasting dimension of the church is evangelical renewal. We have once again to learn how to listen to God and to the world and how to reject the certainties that have clung to the Church from its own past.'[8] He was also able to describe the dynamics of his own theologizing.[9]

The Second Vatican Council has had a great influence on Schillebeeckx. He made many international contacts there which resulted in the creation of the theological journal *Concilium*. The *Tijdschrift Voor Theologie*, which Schilleebeeck also founded, in 1961, and *Concilium*, went further with the reorientation of church and theology which had been prompted by this council.

Vatican II was a new beginning for his own theology. In fact Schillebeeckx dropped all his theological achievements to that point and began to investigate everything again.[10] He carried through the basic theme of the council in his theological thought by entering into dialogue with other disciplines. This had consequences above all for his way of thinking and working. The relationship between God and the world, between tradition and situation, between church and society, has always been the centre of Schillebeeckx's theology. The long Jewish-Christian tradition and all kinds of present-day human experiences form the starting points from which new questions constantly emerge.

II Feminist theology

Feminist theology still has only a short history. As well as the feminist movement of the 1960s, the Second Vatican Council had a part in its origin. The change in views especially about the role of the laity led to the possibility of discussing and thinking through the place of women in church and world. The emancipation of women had a central place.

In the 1960s Catharina Halkes published[11] and spoke a good deal about this. She was one of the few women to be involved in the council. So she wrote an extended paper on the situation of women in the Roman Catholic church for IDOC, the International Documentation Centre which was established in Rome for those taking part in the council and anyone else who was interested. She also spent a month in Rome during each of the first two sessions of the council to write articles for the Dutch newspaper *De Tijd*, specifically about the situation of lay people and the position of women.

She studied Dutch language and literature at Leiden, taught Dutch, and from 1964 was Assistant Director of 'Maartenshof' in Breda, an institute to train laity for pastoral work. In 1970 she became supervisor at the Nijmegen theological faculty. In the meantime she had finished a study on pastoral theology. (Only in the 1960s did it become possible for Catholic women to study theology in the Netherlands.) She was one of the first women to put 'women' on the theological agenda.

Her interest in feminism and theology arose in the Netherlands in the middle of the 1970s. Emancipation and feminism are not the same thing: women who want emancipation want half the existing cake; feminists want a quite different cake.[12] The emancipation of women does not go further than equal rights and duties to those of men and is content with that; it does not criticize these rights, duties, values and norms themselves.[13]

Catharina Halkes was also a pioneer in the sphere of feminist theology in Dutch Catholic theology. She was the first person to bring together feminism and theology. From the beginning she saw feminism and feminist theology as a criticism of culture and religion. American feminist theologians inspired her in this.

To begin with she gave only a few lectures, but from 1977 these were supplemented by a special brief to investigate and teach about 'feminism and Christianity', and in 1983 she became professor of feminism and Christianity.

She has defined feminist theology as a critical theology of liberation which is not based on the uniqueness of women as such but on their historical experience of suffering, their psychological and sexual oppression, infantilization and structural invisibility as a result of sexism in the churches and society.[14]

To begin with, the emphasis was on an exchange of women's experiences of faith and their awareness of them. The whole sphere of theology was the subject for reflection. In the meantime various trends, positions and specializations have developed in feminist theology and there has been more interest in the methods of feminist theological investigation. So it is really better to speak of feminist theologies in the plural, all of which have arisen out of criticism of the way in which women are made invisible and suppressed, but develop in different ways.

The works of Catharina Halkes show a recognizable development[15] from an emancipated woman involved in the church to a critical feminist theologian.[16] However, the Jewish-Christian tradition remains the starting point. Her concern is to enrich existing theology on the one hand by bringing out and expressing what is implicitly present in the Christian tradition, yet has remained hidden as the result of its one-sidedly male content, and on the other by introducing new experiences and reflecting on them.[17]

The experiences of women from the present and the past thus not only enrich theology but also change it. The perspective is now that of women, and there is reflection on the relationship between God and human beings in the light of women's experiences: this has consequences for both the content of theology and the way in which theology is done.

III About Mary

There is a striking silence in theological literature about Mary from the end of the 1960s. In the Netherlands the decline in publications was particularly marked, but a similar tendency could also be detected elsewhere. Marian congresses everywhere were more modest in size.[18]

It is no coincidence that this silence prevailed after the Second Vatican Council. The council started off the discussion about Mary.

Slowly but surely a scepticism had arisen about some mariological exaggeration from this time.[19] Everything still seems to have been fine in 1950, at the time of the declaration of the dogma of the Assumption of Mary, but under the surface something was going on. Mary had suddenly become a problem. That was clear during the council discussions about Mary.[20]

In order to put the problems in context it is necessary to make a few remarks about the prehistory.

Although scripture says little specific about Mary, a wealth of properties, privileges and honorific titles are attributed to her. Here the motto was 'Never enough about Mary'. In the period before the council this was very much the case. Veneration of Mary was very important for many believers. These practices developed even independently of church teaching.[21] But it is striking that the two dogmas about Mary were proclaimed in the nineteenth and twentieth centuries.

From the church side there had been relatively few 'official' statements about Mary. The first was the confession of the Council of Ephesus (431) that Mary is rightly called mother of God. However, the issue in these statements was not Mary; their context was discussion about the right way to think about Christ. The doctrine of her virginity was the second statement about Mary and from of old had been an element in the Apostles' Creed.

In 1854 the dogma of the Immaculate Conception (Mary is without original sin) was proclaimed and in 1950 the dogma of the Assumption of Mary.[22] Really only the latter dogma has to do with Mary herself. Her virginity and immaculate conception are also clearly connected with Christ.

These pronouncements by the church, and also the many devotional practices, raise many questions which cannot be discussed here.

The motto became 'More than enough about Mary'; on the rebound, Catholics turned radically away from Mary when they became aware of this exaggeration. For the first ten or fifteen years after the council people found it difficult to achieve a new balance in mariology. New ways were sought, but people found it hard to get away from the tradition in which Mary's glories were celebrated almost excessively. The critical sobriety of the theologians was difficult to reconcile with popular belief, in which veneration of Mary is strongly associated with belief in appearances and miracles.[23] However, there was more interest on the Protestant side. People rediscovered parts of scripture which had barely functioned for a long time.[24]

After the Second Vatican Council, the sometimes excessive devotion to Mary among Catholics waned and Mary came to occupy the sober place which scripture shows us; the Reformation churches arrived at the insight that they had neglected Mary as a female figure in the history of redemption.[25] But that was not the end of the story.

New impulses arose at the end of the 1970s and during the 1980s. Thus liberation theology from Latin American found the Magnificat an important guideline for interpreting the process of liberation and popular devotion.[26] However, the greatest impulse came from feminist theology.

That is really quite logical. Mary represents the central theme in the history of the Western attitude to women.[27] Criticism of the figure of Mary is at the same time criticism of a view of women. Women discovered that the figure of Mary as they experienced it is different from that of the official church tradition. They found that Mary was very close to them; many women felt accepted and understood by her.[28]

At the same time Mary was played off against women as the woman in the background, the lowly and virginal figure who should be the model for all women.[29]

This ambivalence led to a great variety of views about Mary in feminist theologies. For a number of feminist theologians the misuse of the figure of Mary is enough reason to put her on one side. But more and more theologians are beginning to steep themselves in Mary. Roughly speaking these can be divided into two trends: some see Mary as a survival of the old Mother Goddess from pre-Christian religions; others stress that Mary is an ordinary believer and look within the Christian tradition for 'another' Mary.[30]

Thus discussion about Mary is again in full flow, but as a result of the developments of Vatican II and feminist theology in an essentially different way from the 'quiet period'.

Catharina Halkes and Edward Schilleebeeckx, each in their own way, show how their thought about Mary has changed under the influence of these developments.

Mary then

Schillebeeckx shows through an account of the discussions in and around the Second Vatican Council how views of Mary clashed with each other.

There was a church or church-theological mariology in which Mary was seen as our sister, an eminent and model member of the church's community of faith; and there was a christological mariology which put Mary alongside Jesus Christ to such a degree that Mary – mother of Jesus, who is at the head of his redeemed church – is also called 'mother of the church'.

The first view was that of the majority and was also supported by Schillebeeckx. Schillebeeckx developed this view in the writing and rewriting of his book *Mary Mother of the Redemption* (originally *Mary, Christ's Most Beautiful Creation*, Antwerp 1954).

In his article he looks back critically on this work and in it already sees the two views of Vatican II interwoven in his insights and standpoints. But the first view is already present in the 1950s.

Thus he mentions the quest of the historical Mary on the basis of scripture and the dangers attached to the one-sided bestowal of the title 'mother' on Mary. The most important insight is the role of Mary in redemption; Mary must not be put on the side of Jesus Christ but on the side of the community of faith which is on the receiving end.

Halkes also looks back on her own work about Mary, from the 1960s, but begins yet one stage earlier. She describes what Mary meant in her youth and how Mary became a shadow in her existence: there was only one model, namely the chaste and lowly virgin Mary. She shows how anger and alienation got the upper hand. In the 1960s a change came. Another theological view of Mary brought a quite different Mary to the fore: not Mary the chaste mother but Mary the first among believers. New insights into the biblical context, the significance of Mary in redemption, the significance of Mary's virginity and humanity and the connection between talk about 'Mary' and 'women' played a major role in these publications.

Mary now

After these publications, for Halkes Mary disappeared from the theological scene for a while, but since the 1970s she has again been fully present as a result of developments in feminist theology. Halkes gives a personal and interim account of a quest for the significance of Mary *for women and men* aimed at removing ambiguities from Christian faith. She does this by combining the feminist theological critique with different perspectives like those of ecumenism, Latin American liberation theology, the psychology of religion and depth psychology.

So Mary can become the image of the person who has come closest to the divine in Christianity. Virgin and mother also take on another significance as Mary is seen as the symbol of openness to the mystery of our existence and of prophetic power. Mary has become a sister rather than a mother.

Schillebeeckx points out that the insights from ecumenism and feminist theology have been of great importance for a new view of Mary, but he does not develop this further. Above all he goes into exegesis, which has also played a major role in developments within thought about Mary. His most important conclusion is that the relationship between the Holy Spirit, Mary and the church on the basis of scripture and tradition must be thought out again. The Holy Spirit is the source of all life, including that of the church. Schillebeeckx points out that while titles which are given to Mary had indeed been given earlier to the church, they were originally titles of the Holy Spirit. He then works out his own present-day view of Mary on the basis of a sermon about Mary. He shows how in scripture Mary emerges as the 'mother of all believers'.

Mariology: Yesterday, Today, Tomorrow

Edward Schillebeeckx

In October 1990 the generalate of the Dominican order in Huissen in the Netherlands organized an international congress for members of the order on the subject of 'Mary'.

The organizers asked me to give a short, succinct sketch of the development in my theological thought over the past forty years about the place of Mary in God's system of salvation of Jesus, confessed by the Christian churches as the Christ – from my first specifically mariological publications, especially on the occasion of the pre-Vatican Marian Year in 1954, and then through the Second Vatican Council down to the present day, 1990. They also asked me to describe my present views on the future of mariology, sketched out on the basis of the Bible against the background of my christological trilogy.[1]

I shall take as my starting point the Second Vatican Council, which inserted a concise mariology as the final chapter of its dogmatic constitution *Lumen Gentium*.

I. *Lumen Gentium*, chapter 8: a middle way between mariologial minimalism and maximalism

On the advice of many theologians the majority of the council fathers wanted to have a mariological 'moratorium', a kind of cooling-off process. For many Catholics the declaration of the dogma of the Assumption of Mary in 1950 was not wholly satisfactory. Moreover the Marian Year in 1954 which emerged from it was organized one-sidedly by 'Rome'. People said that marian theology was being overdone by more and more 'mariologists' who wanted a kind of independent marian dogmatics.

The desire of some bishops to see a new dogma proclaimed by this council relating to Mary as *co-redemptrix* in the 'objective redemption'[2] by Christ had the opposite effect on many council fathers. Moreover many non-Catholic, Christian 'observers' (who were very active at this council) were very hesitant about further new definitions of marian dogma. The conservative-theological, extreme positions strengthened the anti-maximalist attitude of the majority of the Catholic council fathers.

So there were two contrasting positions in views about Mary. They came face to face in the discussion of the scheme on Mary. In preparation for the council a separate 'schema'[3] on Mary had been presented, a preliminary conciliar outline apart from, and outside, the schema 'on the church',[4] which was prepared by another commission.

First session: pragmatic discussion

During the first session no real theological discussion of marian doctrine began on the basis of theoretical theological questions, though this was to develop in the second and third sessions.

The beginning of the very first discussion was purely pragmatic. For in the first session of the council, a week before its scheduled end, the final discussion on the Constitution on the Liturgy had been completed. There was just a week before the conclusion of the first session, on 8 December 1962 (a feast of Mary).

The question was, should the one remaining week be devoted to the longer schema 'On the church', or was it not more effective to begin on the brief schema 'On Mary'?

In one week, some people thought, the 'marian doctrine' prepared by 'Rome' could be disposed of, since it was not controversial.

However, other bishops had objections in principle here. They saw this decision, which definitely made sense in pragmatic terms, as implicitly already being a specific and important theological decision. For the majority of the bishops wanted a doctrine of Mary simply included as a sub-section of the dogmatic constitution

'On the church' and not as a separate dogmatic constitution 'On Mary', of the kind that had been prepared in the pre-conciliar scheme. As would emerge at the time of the second session, this was the desire of the majority. The minority wanted a marian doctrine which stood above and indeed outside the church and thus would not be a chapter within a dogmatic constitution 'On the church'. The result of the vote on this problem was that priority must be given to the discussion of 'the church'. This later became the dogmatic constitution *Lumen Gentium*. So the plan of the minority seemed to have failed.

Second session: dogmatic discussion

In 1963, at the second session of the council, a separate schema on Mary was presented for official discussion. Now indeed there was a dogmatic discussion: does the doctrine of Mary have to be handled within the dogmatic constitution on the church or outside it?

Only the title was suddenly changed – no one knows by whom or why. In the documents still being distributed in November 1962 and up to April 1963, the title was specifically: *Schema constitutionis Dogmaticae de Beata Maria Virgine, mater dei et mater hominum* ('Schema for a Dogmatic Constitution on the Blessed Virgin Mary, mother of God and of human beings'). Now the title ran: 'On the Blessed Virgin Mary, the mother of the church'. By changing the title, a minority of the council, above all from Vatican circles, wanted to make another prior theological decision. Although the majority did not think that the title 'Mary, mother of the church' was *per se* illegitimate, their view was that this put Mary too much 'above' and 'outside' the church.

In an even emotional situation, Cardinal König from Vienna had the task of putting forward a proposal on the question whether the constitution on Mary should be worked out independently or should become a sub-section of ecclesiology, the doctrine of the church, the final chapter of *Lumen Gentium*.

The cardinal personally consulted many theologians, advisers to a variety of episcopal conferences. With the Dutch ecumenical theologian, Mgr Jan Groot, I was invited to see him. We advised him: 'First, the "doctrine of Mary" must become a chapter of *Lumen Gentium*, within its ecclesiology, and secondly, the title "Mary, mother of the church" must be avoided'.

We heard later that other theologians advised the same thing. A proposal to this effect, presented by Cardinal König to the plenary assembly, that the doctrine of Mary should be included within the constitution on the church, was approved by a large majority.

Third session: Mary, mother of the church?

In the third session (1964), the central question was whether Mary must be called 'mother of the church'. On 29 October this was rejected by the council with a majority of 1559 votes. There were only 24 votes explicitly in favour of again including the title 'Mary, mother of the church', and 521 votes proposed all kinds of amendments. In the meantime (March, July, October, and also later 21 November 1964) the officially approved title remained *De Beata Maria Virgine Deipara in mysterio Christi et Ecclesia*, a literal translation of which is 'On the blessed God-bearing Virgin Mary in the mystery of Christ and the church'. It is already evident from this that the relationship of Mary to the mystery of Christ was seen by the majority of the council as the foundation of her (sisterly) relationship to the church.

However, the contrasts in mariological views continued to the end of the council. Because the council forthrightly rejected the new title, 'Mary, mother of the church', which had been introduced surreptitiously, but on the other hand did speak of Mary's 'spiritual motherhood of all believers', Paul VI felt called on to satisfy the minority position in the council in the final gathering of the third session of the council by making Mary 'mother of the church' on his own personal, and thus non-conciliar, authority.

Retrospect

It ultimately becomes clear from an analysis of the eighth chapter of *Lumen Gentium* that – although all parties wanted to avoid both minimalism and maximalism in matters of mariology – two types of marian theology continued to stand side by side at the council. These were, 1. a church or church-theological mariology (the standpoint of the majority): Mary is our sister, an eminent and model member of the church's community of faith; 2. a christological mariology (the standpoint of the minority) which puts Mary alongside Jesus to such a degree that she – the mother of Jesus, who as Christ is head of his redeemed church – is herself also called 'mother of the church'.

Why was Vatican II so cautious about accepting the title 'Mary, mother of the church', while the pope, evidently unconcerned and unhampered by any theological constraints, declared Mary to be 'mother of the church' at the end of this session of the council?[5]

Certainly the non-Catholic, Christian observers at the council had also made objections to what they found the unacceptable use of the term 'Mary, mother of the church'. This also played a part.

But in addition, theologians reported that in the first thousand years of Christianity the term 'Mary, mother of the church' was in fact completely unknown.

It is a mediaeval title for Mary and is used rarely even in this marian time. We find the first evidence of use of this title in the course of the eleventh century, in a work by Pseudo-Ambrose, very probably a text of Berengarius of Tours, and then still with some reserve. For the text 'Because Mary is mother of the church, there she has given it the life which is the head of the church', is sensitively supplemented by the qualification 'Mary is also the daughter of the church, because she is the most eminent member of the church'.[6]

A second witness comes from the thirteenth century: 'So the church is the mother of Mary, and Mary is the mother of the church.'[7] After that, this honorific title for Mary is indeed repeated, but extremely sporadically. A somewhat vague text of Augustine's perhaps stands at the origin of this use of the title in the Middle Ages, sparse as it is.[8]

Given the lapse into a mediaeval title for Mary within what in fact is a mediaeval male celibate veneration of women, the pertinent rejection of the title 'Mary mother of the church' by the council was more than understandable and justified. A progressive council father even made the joke, scornfully, if somewhat tastelessly: 'If Mary is called mother of the church, then Mary is at the same time the grandmother of all individual believers.'

II My theological thought about Mary before and after Vatican II

In connection with the Marian Year of 1954 I gave lectures on the place of Mary in the Christian system of salvation to priests who that year would have to preach repeatedly about Mary. I later brought these lectures together, and they first appeared under the title 'Mary, Christ's Most Beautiful Creation' (Antwerp 1954). In the second and subsequent editions (and in all translations) I called it *Mary, Mother of the Redemption*. I took the new title from Aelred of Rievaulx, a mediaeval theologian.[9]

Moreover, at the end of the Second Vatican Council I wrote an article on Mary for an American book on Mary in connection with a post-Vatican, American Rosary Crusade. Not least because of the content of my article at that time, this book on Mary never appeared.

All this raises the question: are there differences worth mentioning between my mariological thought before the council and that after it?

'New' insights

Precisely because, as a result of my book on Mary, which appeared in 1954 and after that was translated into a variety of languages, along with other theologians I had an influence on the eighth chapter of *Lumen Gentium*, it is difficult to speak of my 'pre-Vatican' thought about Mary as compared with my 'post-Vatican' views.

For me the break comes not between 'pre'- and 'post'-Vatican II, but in my pre-Vatican period, especially between the first and second and subsequent editions of the book in question.

It is worth noting that in the second edition I inserted a completely new first chapter. Instead of beginning with 'The Place of the Mother of God in the Christian System of Salvation' (the title of the first chapter in the first edition), from the second edition onwards there was now a completely new chapter with the title 'The Gospel Picture of the Mother of Jesus'.

Just as, much later, after the Second Vatican Council, before analysing the christological confession, I would first investigate precisely what and who the phenomenon of 'Jesus of Nazareth' was, so at the end of 1955 I investigated the historical phenomenon of 'Miriam' ('Mariam' in the Aramaic spoken by Jesus and Mary), the Jewish mother of Jesus of Nazareth. Then already the question was: is the Madonna of Catholic mariology the same as the Jewish Mariam, mother of Jesus? Much later, in recent years, this quest for the historical Mary has been extended and completed by competent experts.[10]

But my new, first, chapter did not go on to have a sufficiently consistent effect on the other chapters of the second and later editions of my book on Mary. Even more strongly than in the first edition the emphasis was placed on the fact that we are redeemed *only through God* in Jesus Christ. In the face of the mariological tendencies which were dominant at that time, to give Mary a place in so-called 'objective redemption', I stressed that Mary must not be put on the side of Jesus Christ but on the side of reception by the community of faith. Later this also became a central affirmation of the mariology of Vatican II.

Because of the attempt to 'keep Mary on our side', at that time I preferred not to use the title 'Mary co-redemptrix' which was current in marian circles at that time, and preferred vaguer references like 'companion in redemption'. That applies to her, as it applies to all Christian believers who through their *fiat* of faith enter into the state of redemption and, being redeemed, in return, by virtue of this grace of redemption, also become grace for others. This universal Christian law of solidarity applies in a unique, eminent, exemplary way to Mary. I said there: 'As the one who stands behind us in the long line of the redeemed, the Mother of God occupies a pre-eminent place. She is not simply one particularly important fellow member of the Mystical Body, but someone who is far more close and intimate – as the mother of the whole Christ, the head of all the members of Christ's mystical body.'[11]

So at that time my basic view was: 'The mother of God is the most sublime human being of all and the firstfruit of Redemption . . .'[12]

The removal of Mary from so-called 'objective redemption' is of course a new step in mariology, but it is not enough. Moreover I pointed out then that from the theological side a critical attitude continued to be necessary even then to 'the many names' which popular devotion gives to Mary.

A mediaeval Dominican, an unknown pupil of Albert the Great, pseudo-Albert, wrote: 'We do not aim to adorn the glorious virgin with our lies.'[13]

St Bernard, a warm mediaeval venerator of Mary, wrote, 'The royal virgin has no need of false honour,'[14] and Bonaventura commented: 'Richly endowed as Mary is with true glory, she can well do without our lies.'[15]

Thomas Aquinas also takes his place in this series of critical marian theologians. He says: 'My verdict is that people do better not to use such frivolous things (about Mary) in a sermon, where moreover all kinds of authentic and true things about Mary can be preached.'[16]

The Middle Ages, in which devotion to Mary took off, were thus at the same time the period when theologians put a brake on the popular mariologies of believers and clergy with little theological training and kept them on biblical paths.

In its criticism of marian excesses, my book on Mary followed the line of these critical mediaeval theologians and what a Protestant theologian, Jürgen Moltmann, was to write years after Vatican II: Mary may not be made 'the melting pot for the most divergent religious needs and desires'[17] of pious people. My pre-Vatican mariology expressly opposes 'both ongoing theological or sentimental exaggerations and rationalistic belittling of the mystery of Mariam'- precisely as the Second Vatican Council was to do ten years later.[18]

Pre-Vatican insights with a post-Vatican colouring

On the other hand, in the second and later editions of my book on Mary, above all in the chapter on 'The Mother of the Church and of All Peoples',[19] there are formulations which I would now prefer to avoid, at least in the way in which they are actually expressed. However, the historical irony is that the first edition of my then still classical, but theologically 'open', book on Mary led to my first conflict with the church hierarchy, though then simply on the local level. Moreover it was the later Cardinal Suenens, then still auxiliary bishop of Mechelen, who refused the episcopal *imprimatur* for my book on Mary because in it I defended the position that the historical Mary did not know that her son Jesus was 'the Son of God' in the later sense of the dogma of Nicaea and Chalcedon.[20] The *imprimatur*, the church's permission for publication, was only given to me at a later stage, when I had toned down my text to say that 'Mary had only a very implicit awareness that her son Jesus was the Son of God'.

Three points in my book on Mary from the 1950s, before the Council, seem on first reading to count as theologically (and not just chronologically) pre-Vatican. But on a second reading it will emerge that that is not necessarily the case. At different points 'post-conciliar' insights can already be seen.

1. The immediate involvement of Mary in redemption

The first point relates to the 'immediate involvement of Mary in both objective and subjective redemption'.[21] Here the influence of the Louvain patrologist, Mgr Joseph Levine, who was devotionally also a warm mariologist, can clearly be recognized.

However, the way in which I work this out does not in any way conflict with the basic tenor of my book and with what Vatican II would say later. I say there that Mary's 'active reception of faith' (in this terminology: thus 'standing beside subjective redemption', as I put it elsewhere in the book) gives openness and space to the 'objective redemption', through Christ alone. In this view Mary, despite the ambiguity of the title of that chapter used there, continues to stand on our side of redemption, not on the side of Jesus Christ: 'Mary is the active prototype of the communion of saints redeemed by Christ.'[22] This is precisely the position of the council, and is not pre-Vatican!

2. Mary, mother of the church

The second point again relates to the title of a chapter, namely 'Mary, Mother of the Church and of All Peoples'.[23] I have already said that Vatican II later refused to use the honorific title 'mother of the church' because of possible (though not necessary) maximalist usages. Many theologians, including myself, advised Cardinal König on this.

In feminist theology (which developed explicitly after Vatican II), it is usual not to call Mary 'our mother' but, rightly, 'our sister'. I also did that in my pre-Vatican book about Mary, without, however, putting any emphasis on it. I wanted to base the uniqueness of Mary's being a woman on the insight that God's unique, redeeming love and goodness transcends human male and female love, and in so doing at the same time in an immanent way contains in itself both paternal and male and maternal and female facets of love. Here I referred among other passages to Jer.31.3; Isa.39.14–16; Hos.11.4.

But at that time I drew a very distinctive mariological conclusion from this. I wrote at the time: 'God's maternal quality of mildness, this particularly feminine tenderness, this *quid nesciam* which is the special mark of the mother cannot, however, become explicit as such in the man Jesus. It can only become explicit in a mother who is a woman.'[24]

So Mary was chosen by God to represent the feminine and maternal aspect of God's goodness and love that transcend both man and woman. In itself at the time this was not an unworthy 'argument of convenience'. Quite the contrary, it was very appropriate.

Now one can advance all kinds of anthropological and feminist objections to this. However, at the time the argument had only incidental rather than essential significance for my mariology. But within our situation here and now, this position, if it is maintained, has a much less innocent significance. Certainly after criticisms from ecumenical circles, after the analyses of many feminist theologians and above all after the analysis by E.Drewermann of the link between compulsory celibacy and ties to the mother (which is bewilderingly generalized but essentially on the mark).[25] So in the future we shall have to look for the theological significance of Mary's femininity more along the lines of a sistership which brings freedom than a motherhood which binds the child. I certainly toned down in my book even then the 'spiritual motherhood of Mary towards all believers' (which was later also approved by Vatican II), by saying that 'all Mary's motherly care is directed towards Christ'.[26]

3. The church as mother?

The third point really does not relate to a theologically pre-Vatican standpoint in my book on Mary from that Marian Year but is connected with criticism from ecumenical circles. In that book I call the church itself 'our mother',[27] a term of course which is used a good deal in patristics. Protestant theologians object to this, not without reason. The priestly celibacy which was introduced later gives a complelely new background to the term; then indeed 'the church symbolically becomes mother and believers in religious terms the children of the church',[28] obedient, subjected children, 'tied to their mother'.

However, most of Mary's honorific titles were first ecclesiological titles. From the moment that Mary (rightly) began to be regarded as 'the type' of the redeemed community of faith,[29] it was quite understandable that many ecclesiological titles should be transferred to Mary.

But in the fourth section, below, we shall see that this mariological use of honorific titles is already a further derivation, a derivation of the second order. Not only on ecumenical grounds but moreover on general catholic and ultimately trinitarian and theological grounds, greater theological modesty is called for. But first a word about the veneration of Mary.

III Marian veneration and practice around Vatican II

The legitimacy of a sober veneration of Mary, in popular devotion also, follows from the theological place which Mary occupies in the Christian system of salvation. Morover I defended this in my book from the Marian Year and I still stand by it.

For Catholics, the veneration of the saints is an explicitation of the express experience of Christ. All holiness, including that of Mary, is purely participation in the holiness of God in Christ Jesus. As I said in that book, true religion is 'not a neo-Platonic repentance and conversion to God alone. We meet God himself, a God who is in love with the world, in the very heart of every religious act'[30] (what I was later constantly to call the 'God concerned for humanity' as an expression of the 'kingdom of God' in keeping with the gospel).

So the veneration of Mary is *par excellence* the experience of Christ. However, explicit devotion to Mary presupposes the dogmatic development of the place of Mary in the system of salvation of Jesus Christ. This includes the insight of faith that Mary as a person belongs to the heart of the reality of revelation. Though her *'fiat'* she made possible the human coming of Jesus as redeemer into this world.

The church defends the view that a full-grown and explicitly Christian life also has an essentially marian character. The Reformer Luther also saw that.

The significance of devotion to Mary

However, Vatican II rightly continued to refuse to give explicit and honourable mention to any specific form of devotion to Mary. So the council did not accede to the request made by some council fathers that explicit mention should be made of devotion to the rosary, which is historically so dear to many Dominicans.[31] Particular devotions to Mary, however valuable they may be, remain a matter of choice for Christianity as a whole. And therefore it is good that universal church councils should keep silent about them.

In its Constitution on the Sacred Liturgy, Vatican II has stated that although liturgical prayer is the supreme activity of church life, this does not exhaust the whole of the church's practice of prayer (no.9). The liturgy is indeed the source of all other church activities, and these must in turn be orientated on the liturgy (no.10). However, alongside the liturgy there are other forms of 'application to the spiritual life' (nos.11–13). Liturgical prayer may not suppress extra-liturgical prayer (no.12),

There is an encouraging discussion of non-liturgical popular devotions, on condition that these are co-ordinated with the church's liturgical year, breathe a liturgical spirit, and nourish the liturgical spirit. This applies above all to the devotions that the Apostolic See has approved or are commended by bishops in the local churches. The report (or Relatio) refers to the encyclical *Mediator Dei*, which speaks for example of the Stations of the Cross and the Rosary. However, despite this instruction, this Relatio also seeks expressly to put emphasis on the priority of the liturgy over all paraliturgical devotion, and as an example of non-liturgical popular piety it gives 'a procession in honour of St Anthony at Pentecost'!

The latest development

After the council it was the Apostolic Injunction *Marialis cultus, On the Veneration of Mary*, of Pope Paul VI,[32] which developed Vatican ideas further and in which Mary was expressly called our sister. However, Pope John Paul II's marian encyclical *Redemptoris Mater*[33] (despite many referenes to the marian letter of his predecessor) goes in a quite different direction, and tends more towards the views of the minority at the time of the Second Vatican Council.

IV The future of present-day problems relating to Mary

New questions and new reflection

Present-day exegetical and historical studies of Mary present us with completely new problems. The source of many marian convictions among Christians stem from the so-called Protevangelium of James[34] and other apocryphal works.[35]

This is certainly pious, inward-looking literature with a Christian inspiration, but as well as containing much pious popular fantasy, above all it has clear traces of docetic[36] and gnostic[37] deviations from the gospel.

In particular the 'virgin birth of Jesus', also for historical, biblical and theological reasons, is now interpreted by many theologians in a different way from the literal and biological sense which was understandable in the context of the view of human beings and the world that was taken for granted earlier.

Then there follows the unavoidably real question: must one give Joseph the same honorific tites as Mary, or must one also accord Mary's modest but eminent place as the firstfruit of Christian faith and the firstfruit of the Christian community of faith to Joseph, the righteous husband of Mariam, mother of Jesus?

Before the Second Vatican Council, though for quite different reasons, including the intrinsic consistency of the maximalist mariology of the time, an originally French religious association of priests, called the Oratory, made particular efforts in their Canadian province of St Joseph in the first direction. They were supported by some Dominicans there.

In the infancy narratives of the Gospel of Matthew the birth and infancy of John the Baptist and of Jesus are told from the perspective of Joseph, while Luke relates his story from the perspective of Mary.

Given these complications throughout the classical problems relating to Mary, both from the recent past and in the present, I think that at the moment completely new reflection is needed on the saving figure of Mary.

Within my search for a true, responsibly Christian, authentic christology, I would now, for a start, want to speak of my quest for a pneuma-christological[38] mariology, purely on a New Testament basis.

The Holy Spirit and Mary

What fascinates me theologically today in connection with mariology is this.

The New Testament, and above all the Gospel of John, says that during his earthly life Jesus was completely filled with the Holy Spirit and also acted on the basis of this gift of spiritual fullness in his earthly life. Only 'with Pentecost' – not before and not later – was the Spirit of God, which is the Spirit of Christ, also poured out on the people redeemed by the messianic Jesus.

However, the New Testament makes an exception to this merely Paschal gift of the Spirit. According to the Gospel of Luke the historical Mariam, mother of Jesus, also already receives the Holy Spirit before Pentecost. This is the reason why what is born of her is called holy, 'son of God' (Luke 1.35). In the Gospel, in the New Testament, Mary is the first to share in the history of the Holy Spirit which takes place in our secular history, a real history which is set in motion by Jesus Christ, and her name is associated with his work of salvation.

Of course in Luke 1.15 it is said of John the Baptist too that 'he shall be filled with holy spirit already in his mother's womb', just as it is also said of Elizabeth that 'she will be filled with holy spirit' (Luke 1.41). However, in the case of John the Baptist and Elizabeth this is a provisional 'gift of prophecy'. Moreover it must be conceded that in all these cases, and also in connection with Mary, there is mention only of 'holy spirit' (without an article) and not of 'the Holy Spirit'. And one can hardly translate the greeting 'blessed', which is common (in the Septuagint),[39] as 'full of grace' (in the later theological sense of the word, as the Vulgate[40] will do, though this is a term which Luke uses in connection with Stephen, Acts 6.8). The significance of 'highly favoured' is finally explained by Luke himself (1.30), namely 'find grace with the Lord'. This term appears often in the Old Testament.

However, here it takes on special significance because it is about the exalted grace of being able to be mother of the Messiah. The

26

distinctive feature of the 'transforming of Mary by God through grace' lies in the link between the words 'holy spirit', 'overshadow' and 'come to someone' and the result of all this: the child is 'holy' and 'son of God' (Luke 1.35). *Pneuma hagion* (holy spirit, without an article) in the Old and New Testaments means God's creative power; here too in Luke, 'power of the Almighty' is synonymous with 'holy spirit'. However, when it is connected with verbs like 'come upon someone' (Acts 1.8: 'when you receive power from the Holy Spirit which will come upon you', the same verb as in Luke 1.35; see Isa.32.15), and above all with 'overshadow': cast a shadow on, or let a shadow fall on (as later was the case with Peter, Acts 5.15), and finally with the giving of the name son of God, then all this suggests at the same time the idea of the cloud that veils God's presence.

In his account of the Transfiguration, the story of the change in Jesus' appearance, Luke says: 'A cloud came and overshadowed him' (the same verb, 9.34). In the Old Testament it was a cloud which cast a shadow of God's glory on the tents in the wilderness (Ex.40.35; Num.9.17–22), and 'overshadowing' in general refers to a shadow constantly cast by God's presence and therefore a sign of that presence (Num.10.34; Isa.4.5; Deut.33.12; Ps.91.4, etc.).

In Luke's infancy Gospel there is a divine presence which casts its shadow on Mary. 'Overshadowing by holy spirit' and 'being called son of God' here evoke each other. In this context of Jesus' conception in Mary's womb this certainly does not mean that the Spirit takes over the role of the man in producing a child; what we have here is God's unique presence in the origin of new life, the life of this human child Jesus. Therefore what is coming to be in Mary's womb through God is called 'holy', indeed Son of God. Not in isolation, but in connection with the whole context, above all with the naming of Jesus as 'Son of God', the relationship between Mary and 'holy spirit' here takes on a special meaning. Just as in the pre-Pauline tradition Jesus' 'divine sonship' is connected with the working of the Holy Spirit in Jesus' enthronement through his resurrection (Rom.1.2–4), and just as the term 'Son of God' is connected by the Gospels (also in Luke 3.22; 4.14;

Acts 10.36–38) with Jesus' solemn appointment at his baptism with the visible presence of the Spirit in the form of a dove which overshadows him from above the Jordan with outspread wings, so in the infancy Gospel of Luke it is said that thanks to the 'overshadowing by the Spirit' Jesus is already 'Son of God' at his conception (Luke 1.35). He is Son of God through conception, not through subsequent enthronement, whether at his baptism or at his resurrection.

The Holy Spirit and the church

In the course of church history, above all among the church fathers, a quite distinctive relationship has repeatedly been claimed between Mary and the Holy Spirit, the power of God's presence. Theologically, in itself this is nothing new. But really that idea never becomes an independent theme, in a way which would fit 'real theologizing' today.

Where this does happen explicitly, as it does in a recent book by the liberation theologian Leonardo Boff,[41] the pneumatic relationship which Boff rightly recognizes is seriously exaggerated. He speaks of a 'hypostatic union'[42] between Mary and the Spirit of God, just as there is a hypostatic union between Jesus and the Word or the Logos of God.

I myself am critical of Boff's mariological exaggerations and am also critical of some of the details in my earlier book on Mary. I would now want to say that it is not Mary but the Holy Spirit which is the source of all life, including that of the church. I was well aware of that then, but I did not make it a theme of my mariological publications.

In the light of what for me is now a clear new look (though of course it is old in Christianity), it is not Mary but the Holy Spirit who is 'the mother of all believers', the true 'mother of the church'. The Spirit of God and of Christ is also the wisdom dwelling in the church and the 'shekinah', the indwelling of God's free presence in creation and covenant and church: in Jesus Christ. For if we look deeper into our Christian tradition of faith (which I did in preparing for this lecture to this Dominican symposium, and I am grateful that I stand in that tradition, in fact first unasked and then reflectively and with full and happy freedom), then we discover that even before ecclesiological titles of honour (e.g. the church as the 'ark of the covenant', the 'seat of wisdom', the 'gates of David', the 'refuge of sinners', the 'comforter of the oppressed', etc.) are by mariological transference also bestowed on Mariam, the mother of Jesus (see the Litany of Our Lady), these ecclesiological titles of honour were themselves also transferred from even more original Christian honorific titles for the Holy Spirit – the primal source of all ecclesiological and subsequently mariological transferences. So the mariological titles of honour are a second-level transference. They are transferred from the Holy Spirit to the church, and from this ecclesiological transference 'transferred' once again, specifically to Mary, the mother of Jesus, the first and pre-eminent member in faith of the church's community of faith.

The whole of the church's mariology must therefore be re-actualized on the basis of the fundamental idea that the Holy Spirit is 'mother of the church'. All further transference of pneumatological titles of honour both to the church and to Mary must be reviewed again very critically: pneumatologically and christologically, then ecclesiologically, and finally mariologically.

A 'new' mariology

In the light of what I feel to be an authentic gospel view, faithful to the nucleus of the biblical and post-biblical Christian tradition of faith, we can work out a mariology which is not only post-modern and faithful to the gospel but at the same time up-to-date.

This will be, moreover, a mariology centred on Jesus which can speak meaningfully to present-day, even secularized people. Finally, it will feed a modern marian spirituality, a spirituality of the symbiosis of inwardness and outwardness, an attitude of life which is also turned outwards – to others and to the world. The almost 'revolutionary' and in any case active significance of such a mariology, in which the poor are raised up by God, emerges clearly from the New Testament marian hymn the Magnificat (Luke 1.45–55), which came to poetic life through a pre-Lucan source from the oldest foundations of Jewish Hellenistic Christianity.[43]

V Daring to preach about Mary today

On a ten-minute ride within Nijmegen I constantly get into pastoral conversations with taxi-drivers, whom I now know very well. They now know that I am a priest and a theologian. Some months ago a young driver who had had to wait for me in the reception lobby of the Albertinum asked me, when I had got in his cab, 'That book in the porter's window, *The Schillebeckx Case*, what's it about?' I explained to him some of the difficulties that my books had caused 'Rome'. He knew that there had been problems over my view of Christianity, as he put it. Then he asked, 'What did they find wrong with your books?' I did my very best to explain something of this to him as simply as possible. I said to him: 'Look, you're a Catholic, if I asked you whether you believed that God in the most personal way came to dwell as a human being among us, and a friend of yours, pointing to some passer-by, were to say, "Look, there goes God", what would you think?' The young man didn't have to reflect long and said with a laugh, 'That's absolutely stupid; it's quite crazy.' I was amazed and said, 'What do you mean? You said that you believed in Jesus Christ!' 'Of course,' he replied spontaneously; 'otherwise I wouldn't go to church on Sunday. He is really someone from God. But God in human clothes is too much for me.' I said, 'That was precisely the problem with Rome. You're a real theologian!'

'He is really someone from God.' Can a theologian put it better and more accurately?

I was reminded of this above all when I was asked, 'How do you see Mary now and how would you preach about her?' Many preachers underestimate how much their listeners, the so-called 'simple believers', reflect on faith, and so their sermons are sometimes trivial or unnecessarily learned. Protestant sermons have a tendency to make a category mistake in sometimes confusing the pulpit of proclamation and witness with the platform of academic exegesis, even with an almost mystical use of Hebrew words, as if this language came from God's own mouth. By contrast, Catholic preachers have a tendency not to take the gospel text which they have just read literally enough and simply give a talk round it which has little to do with the text that has been read out. Sometimes they do that in a moving way which is near to life, sometimes they are dry and moralizing, and sometimes also banal or, at the opposite extreme, admirable as literature: but in all these cases after the sermon the congregation is still left with all the questions that the gospel they have heard raises for them. Sometimes there are more questions than experiences of meaning!

The sermon by a woman that I heard recently during a celebration of the eucharist in Advent was a good example of what I would want to do if I had to preach on Mary. So this sermon is also printed at the end of my article.

This sermon begins by taking the infancy gospel as it is. That is how it is read out in the liturgy, and precisely in this form this reading raises all kinds of questions for modern men and women, believers included.

The sermon begins with an unprepossessing picture of mother Mary which the preacher noticed in a church when she was on holiday. Evidently no one was interested in it, while the richly adorned Madonnas, throned in triumph, portrayed on postcards at the back of the church, were snapped up by visitors. One could have said, 'Let the real Mary stand up!' For do we have to do with a heavenly Madonna, or with a young Jewish mother (and in those regions girls can be married at twelve) who with her husband-to-be, like many other pious poor of the time, looked longingly for the liberating Messiah? When the rumours about the itinerant preacher Jesus later went all around Galilee, didn't people ask, 'Isn't that Jesus, the son of Joseph?' (John 6.42), and elsewhere even, 'Surely that is Joseph's son?' (Luke 4.22). The Jewish girl Mariam in fact seems more to resemble the simple picture that was overlooked by the bystanders and was absent from the series of pictures of the heavenly Madonna that were on sale.

The sermon then goes on soberly about the Jewish humanity of Mary since – it is added as a hint – Christians have almost forgotten that the couple, Mary and Joseph, loved each other and that God wanted a human child as a fruit of love.

Without any kind of 'learned' exposition, the sermon clearly tells the hearers that at the time of the historical birth of Jesus there were no shepherds to be seen, nor did wise men come from the East. Nor were there any heavenly songs of praise; perhaps there wasn't even a manger in which the newborn Jesus was laid. That sort of thing certainly happened more in village families, where human beings and domestic animals lived together, and somewhere in a particular corner of the house there was a hollow in the earth or stone wall as a food container – in fact like a trough – for the animals, a small niche that could also serve as what we would now call a cradle for a baby (at all events, not a wooden crib; at that time wood was far too expensive). In the sermon the preacher says all this in a very modest, indirect and careful way.

Where there are biblical stories the historicity of which is at least very improbable, the only correct and appropriate question is how one deals with them. For on the one hand you can certainly deny the firm basis of this story, but if you do that, on the other hand you may immediately give someone hearing that story the impression that God's guidance, which is spoken of in the story in connection with the newborn Jesus, is just as much a fiction and an illusion.

As believers, Christians are at the same time modern men and women who have gone through the phase of critical historical questioning. And we cannot and may not keep quiet about that piece of life in and of ourselves and shut it up. To keep quiet about the historical question would be an ostrich policy, unworthy of truly Christian belief here and now. No sensible person can historically deny the fundamental fact that Mary was the mother of Jesus. That is the historical foundation of everything that can be said critically about Mary in a meaningful way. She is thus the mother of someone who was later confessed by Christians as the liberator, the redeemer, the one who bears the sin of the world, but was done away with by human beings because his disarming love seemed dangerously threatening above all to those who were put in authority. However, God chose the side of a love which was disarming and disarmed, and therefore also vulnerable and indeed rejected. He put his seal, his divine hall-mark, on the life of a man who was captivated by the kingdom of God in the form of justice and love among human beings and peoples, a kingdom without domination or tyranny. That in particular was extremely threatening for those in authority, who could only maintain their power by oppression and tyranny. Jesus' life, rejected by human beings, was accepted by God as the life and work of his dearest son. This was confessed of the historical person, Jesus of Nazareth, by his followers.

Precisely because of the divine acceptance of which the believing Easter experience of the disciples is simply a reflection in the dimension of our history, the followers of Jesus again began to reflect on him and later (for the Gospel of Mark and the Johannine tradition from which the Fourth Gospel was to be born do not have an infancy story) also on his mother.

With its perspective back from later belief the simple sermon offered in this book also made a right decision. In the light of the ultimate belief in the resurrection of Mary's son, the heavenly voices, the shepherds and the wise men from the East belong in a miraculous and essential way to the story of Jesus' birth: in the historically obscure, even anonymous, event of Mary's child, historically unknown, God (historically) brings about the birth of the one whom Jewish followers of Jesus later called the 'messianic son of David' and his Hellenistic followers the *soter* or the 'saviour and benefactor' (a term given in the Hellenistic world to the Roman emperor): the historical Jesus is the saviour of Jews and all peoples, of all humanity.

In retrospect, that is what the two infancy stories (in Matthew and Luke) mean to make clear; in connection with Jesus' birth, both of them are narratives, narrative commentaries on Christian belief which is already long past. In these birth stories Luke and Matthew certainly do not seek to provide an account of the historical events around the birth of Jesus. In that story the historical character of the Jewish child that is born of Mary is retained and kept safe, but at the same time to the eyes of later

Christian belief this birth seems far to transcend in its depth dimension the simple and visible event of an ordinary birth of the kind that also took place in the house of Mary and Joseph: at that time (although believers only knew this around thirty years later), it was no less than the birth of Jesus Christ 'our Lord'.

Mary, the mother of all belief

If I reflect further on Mary and scripture I come to the following conclusions, prompted first by the reaction of Jesus to his mother, and second by the veneration of Mary in the earliest community of faith. I shall try to illuminate this as briefly as possible here, though I would prefer to present all my findings, arguments and questions so that it becomes clearer on what grounds I come to my conclusions.

A. The reaction of Jesus to his mother

It is striking how in the first three so-called Synoptic Gospels (of Matthew, Mark and Luke) Jesus reacts to the message 'Look, your mother and your brothers and sisters are outside seeking you' (Mark 3.31–35; Matt.12.45–50; Luke 8.18–21). Pointing to his disciples, who follow him wherever he goes, Jesus answers in the three Gospels: 'Look, here are my mother and my brothers. For whoever does the will of my Father in heaven, he is my brother and sister and mother' (Matt.); 'Anyone who does the will of God is my brother and my sister and my mother' (Mark); 'My mother and my brothers are those who hearken to the word of God and do it' (Luke).

Is Mary here praised in passing by Jesus, her son, not so much for her biological motherhood of the Messiah as for her attitude of faith, her hearing and doing of the word of God? Or is she being discreetly rejected, while Jesus' disciples, who follow him everywhere (whereas Mary clearly does not belong to the group of disciples and women who 'follow' him), are made the model of the true disciple and believer?

On Jesus' side a certain distance from his own family in religious

34

matters is understandable and really even essential for his calling. For him, what comes first is what he himself sees as the consequence of a calling which has been offered and accepted: 'Anyone who puts his hand to the plough and looks back is not fit for the kingdom of God' (Luke 9.62). This model of one called by God, which is also respected by Jesus, is described in its authentic, even rough, originality in Deut.33.9–10, and this theme resounds throughout the Gospel witness, which speaks of listening to God's word and doing it. Before his death Moses, the man of God, blesses all the Israelites (Deut.33.1). He says of the tribe of Levi and his tribal ancestor (chosen for levitical service): 'Who said of his father and mother"I regard them not"; and he disowned his brothers and ignored his children. For they observed thy word, and kept thy covenant' (Deut 33.9–10). Basically this is the same attitude as we find Jesus adopting towards his family for the sake of his message of the kingdom of God (this attitude in no way excludes inward love of parents and the observance of the Ten Commandments, especially, 'You shall love your father and mother', but it can at least transcend the letter of the law). Jesus calls for the same attitude from disciples who want to follow him: 'Whoever loves father and mother more than me is not worthy of me' (Matt.10.37–38, cf. also John 12.25). Luke himself puts it even crudely, like this: 'If anyone comes to me and does not hate his own father and mother and wife and children and brothers and sisters, yes, and even his own life, he cannot be my disciple' (Luke 14.26). Elsewhere it is said that anyone who thus leaves his family for the sake of the kingdom of God will be recompensed one hundredfold (Luke 18.29–30; Mark 10.28–29).

The words sound harsh, but for Jesus they mean that you must unconditionally give up everything for the kingdom of God; this commitment has priority over the rest. A certain distancing of Jesus from his family, not so much affectively and emotionally, as for the sake of the kingdom of God, is historically difficult to deny.

Against the background of the real or possible gossip among some members of the family (evidently those in authority) who regard Jesus as a fanatic, Jesus' mother, Mariam, to the degree that the four masculine Gospels pay her any special attention, is in fact depicted as a mother and a woman who ponders everything in her heart: both all the pros and cons which were evidently the subject of discussion in her own family. The Gospels give the impression that Mary did not find her solitary faith in God easy, did not find it easy to be the mother of this Jesus about whom so much dispute had meanwhile arisen in the Jewish world. The manifestly ambiguous assessment of Jesus affected his deeply believing Jewish mother in a special way, since she did not understand what her son was really concerned about. At all events, she did not belong to the group of women which followed her son on all his itinerant preaching (Luke 8.1–3: we do not know the whys or wherefores). At least according to the Synoptic Gospels, even less did she belong to the group of women who had followed Jesus from Galilee on his journeys and who were the only ones, unlike Jesus' male disciples, to be present, albeit at a distance, at the crucifixion of Jesus (Mark 15.40–41; Matt.27.55–56; Luke 23.49). According to the Synoptic Gospels and also according to the later special scraps of tradition which are known only to Matthew and Luke respectively (what exegetes call the Matthaean and Lukan 'special material'), Mary is absent throughout the whole public ministry of Jesus, and absent even at the historical conclusion of Jesus' life on the cross.

Only the Gospel of John has the mother of Jesus present at the cross, immediately below it: 'But standing by the cross of Jesus were his mother, and his mother's sister, Mary the wife of Clopas, and Mary Magdalene. When Jesus saw his mother, and the disciple whom he loved standing near, he said to his mother, "Woman, behold your son!" Then he said to the disciple, "Behold your mother!" And from that hour the disciple took her to his own home' (John 19.25–27).

The much-disputed question about the historicity of Mary's standing beneath the cross of Jesus continues to preoccupy me, despite the fact that the Synoptics are unanimous in their testimony that Mary was not present there. I would therefore venture a guess which presupposes that (given the Gospel of John) we must reckon that it was at least possible that Mary was present under the cross, however problematical this may remain. However, I shall not go more deeply here into the questions connected with this, but develop my view quite briefly. First of all it must be noted that Mary was certainly not among the group of women who went with Jesus to Jerusalem and there took part in the events surrounding Jesus' arrest and execution from afar. The Synoptics are unanimous in excluding Mary from the public life of Jesus – apart from one text according to which his mother and his brothers came to look for him. However, apart from Mark (3.21), if we must at least relate Mark 3.21 to Mark 3.31, not a word is said about why his mother and his family came to look for Jesus and what they had to say to him. And this indicates that the literary presence of his mother and his brothers in the story simply serves to illustrate what Jesus says: here, these, my followers, are my mother, sisters and brothers.

On this presupposition my guess goes like this. We know of Mary that she was a Jew who observed the law. Unless we want to concede an illegitimate mistake in chronology, in the first instance it is hard to imagine Mary historically during the public life of Jesus as 'the first Christian'! Mary's Jewish observance of the law must be the starting point for all Christian reflections on her. In that case it cannot be ruled out historically that she too (of course independently of the group of women who met with Jesus in Jerusalem for the Passover, the feast whch commemorated Israel's exodus from Egypt) came to Jerusalem in a group with some friends and acquaintances, as was the custom then, to celebrate the passover. Since she was a Jew, this would have been quite natural. Now that same passover week the sentence on Jesus was carried out. If she stayed in Jerusalem, could she have failed to hear what was happening to her son, who had been condemned to crucifixion? In that case her presence and certainly not 'far off', but as it were immediately under the cross, is plausible and humanly imaginable.

Nevertheless, for me that is not a serious argument; it is too speculative. However, I have yet another pointer from another source, namely the Lukan tradition. After the death of Jesus and the earliest development of belief in Jesus' resurrection among the first 'Christian' believers, in his Acts Luke relates how the disciples of Jesus waited in prayer in an upper room somewhere in Jerusalem for the coming of the promised Spirit. And Luke writes: 'All these (the apostles) with one accord devoted themselves to prayer, together with the women and Mary the mother of Jesus, and with his brothers' (Acts 1.14).

So I do not think the presence of Mary under the cross impossible as a historical fact. And if this indeed was the case, this fact is a surprising, almost unexpected, confirmation of all that a critical analysis of what the New Testament says about Mary as 'the mother of all belief' is in a position to state, with our modern difficulties but nevertheless in responsible belief.

According to Jesus, throughout the New Testament belief in God's word and doing what that word says is the foundation of being his disciple. If Mary, his mother, is also praised by Jesus, this will be because she has heard and held fast to the word of God. As will become clear in due course, the Christian 'community of God' which had just come into being understood that well, and that is and remains the foundation of any veneration of Mary and any mariology.

B. The veneration of Mary in the earliest Christian community

Mothers of great historical figures in any sphere get a special place of honour in the memory of the people in question. This is a deeply human event, a kind of primal experience which led a woman who (at least according to the one witness in the Gospel of Luke) listened to a saying of Jesus to cry out spontaneously. 'As he said this, a women in the crowd raised her voice and said to him, "Blessed is the womb that bore you, and the breasts that gave you suck" ' (Luke 1.27). This reaction, coming from a tradition which is special to Luke, is not just an authentic and general human reaction, but in addition is specifically typical of Judaism, especially in connection with the mother of the coming Messiah (in the Gospels themselves, Luke 1.43, but also in many other Jewish texts).

And in his reaction to the outburst of this woman Jesus himself in no way seeks to brush off or deny her praise. However, he puts a critical question-mark against it. For him, biological motherhood cannot be the occasion for beatitudes about his mother. Luke, the only one of the evangelists to refer to the witness of a woman from the crowd, makes Jesus react like this: 'But he said,"In fact, blessed are those who hear the word of God and keep it (hold it fast)" ' (Luke 11.27). This phrase 'in fact', which is rightly inserted into modern translations, nevertheless, by general consent, gives quite a different turn to the woman's spontaneous remark. Moreover Luke explains Jesus' parallel of the seed that fell on good soil like this: 'And as for that in the good soil, they are those who, *hearing the word, hold it fast* in an honest and good heart, and *bring forth fruit* with patience' (Luke 8.15): hear it and hold it fast and because of that 'bring forth fruit' – the same words as in Luke 11.27 (see also Luke 1.42–43). Thanks to Mary's hearing God's word and holding it fast, in other words thanks to Mary's *fiat* in faith and action, Jesus is indeed 'the blessed fruit of her womb'.

Moreover Luke has Mary reacting to the message of the angel like this: ' "Behold the handmaid of the Lord, be it to me according to what you say" ("let it happen to me according to your word"). Then the angel went away' (Luke 1.3). In Mary, listening to God's word in faith and doing it go hand in hand. That is what she is praised for by Jesus implicitly in Luke 11.27.

However, what counts for Jesus is not the biological side of her motherhood, on which the woman from the crowd seems to put the stress, but the consistent expression of belief in God in action. It is from that in particular that devotion to Mary in the early church arose, even before the scriptures.

From the analysis of the two infancy narratives I learn that the main title among other possibly legitimate titles of Mary, at least in the first instance, is based on the fact that historically she is the 'mother of Jesus'. This is the basic condition for the possibility of calling her 'mother of Christ' and finally 'mother of the Lord'

(Luke 1.43) at a later stage, when belief in who and what Jesus of Nazareth really means for believers had developed and even been made explicit. In other words, the foundation for all the honorific titles of Mary lay in the fact that, or rather in the believing way in which, she became the 'mother of Jesus of Nazareth', the mother of the one whom Christians confess as 'the messianic Son of Man, God's own beloved Son, our Lord'. That is not only the foundation for all recognition of particular legitimate honorific titles for Mary, but also the necessary limit to them. This already implies some criticism of a widespread saying of certain mariologists who continue to repeat '*de Maria numquam satis*', one can never speak highly enough of Mary. But! In the person of Mary herself one can go beyond prescribed boundaries and obscure Christian belief by too much of a good thing, by projecting all human wishes and frustrations on mother Mary, making her almost even more than Jesus the solution to all problems. Even Jesus is not that, despite the understandable sigh of St Augustine, '*Jesus solutio omnium difficultatum*', Jesus the solution of all difficulties! The Gospels also support me in both indicating legitimate reasons and laying down necessary limits for a true and legitimate devotion to Mary. For it can always be said that the mystery of a person can never be exhausted in words.

The reaction to Mary on the part of both Jesus and the early church amounts to praise both of the true believer and of the *model* of the true believer sketched out by Jesus himself, the splendour and glory of which is projected on to the figure of Mary as the believing mother of this Jesus. Mary is the living embodiment of this model. As a kind of antitype of Abraham, the father of all belief, Mary emerges as the model of all faith in the New Testament specifically as a mother. This is no small praise of the believing mother of Jesus, a true gift of God. And of course etymologically Mariam means 'gift of God', a rare name at an earlier stage, but one which was frequently given to women in Judaism where a Moses mysticism was alive in memory of Miriam, the sister of Aaron, who sang the refrain of the great song after the crossing of the Sea of Reeds (Ex.15.20).

The pre-Lucan hymn the Magnificat, taken up by the Gospel of Luke and adapted here and there to fit its theological view, confirms all this, and as a hymn of praise to God is itself already a witness to living devotion to Mary, even before Luke wrote his gospel. The basis for this veneration lies both in the fact that Mary is the mother of the Messiah Jesus (Luke 1.42) and, essentially bound up with this, in her unshakable faith: 'And blessed is she who believed that there would be a fulfilment of what was spoken to her from the Lord' (Luke 1.45). This is an important fact: it is testimony to the existence of an early Christian veneration of Mary and indicates the reason why this came about. Mary is the mother of Jesus, the Messiah, our Lord, and she is the model for all belief in God. Alongside Abraham, the father of all belief, she is the mother of all belief.

The Magnificat from the Gospel of Luke is, moreover, the first undoubted expression of devotion to Mary in the earliest church. Verse by verse this Magnificat is composed of implicit quotations from the Old Testament (and the author also knows the Song of Hannah, I Sam.2.1–10). This hymn of praise to God is the first great expression of Christian devotion to Mary. Luke is also the one who indicates the basis of this veneration in the welcome given to Mary by Elizabeth, which shows how much Christian reflection has already grown up in the meantime: 'Blessed are you among women, and blessed is the fruit of your womb! And why is this granted me, that the mother of the Lord should come to me?. . . . Blessed is she who believed' (Luke 1.42–43, 45).

This indicates the foundation of all true veneration of Mary:

1. Mary is the mother of Jesus.
2. She is to be praised above all for her belief.
3. She is really already called 'mother of God'. Elizabeth says 'the mother of my Lord'; this word 'my' in this connection can hardly refer to Christos Kyrios (although Luke does use this one term throughout his infancy gospel), but certainly does not fit into the mouth of Elizabeth at that moment: the hymn clearly means 'of my God' (the Jewish name for Adonai, the unutterable name of God).
4. The marked effect of the communication of the divine pneuma.

41

In that case, in my view, in the term 'mother of all belief' we have the real main and original title for Mary – a title which both offers an opening and sets limits – as the foundation for an authentic veneration of Mary. Moreover we have to work out a mariology which keeps to biblical criteria.

Given the four New Testament criteria I have just mentioned, true veneration of Mary is part of the essence of Christianity, within which Jesus Christ alone, intent on the one God of all human beings, himself showing the way to the one God of all human beings, may be named the centre and focus. Mary, the mother of this Jesus, the Christ, Son of God, or Lord, reflects in her believing dedication something of the splendour of her son Jesus Christ. Alongside Abraham, Mary – as the believing mother of Jesus, confessed by Christians as Christ, God's Son, our Lord – is the mother of all believers.

Thoughts about Celebrating Christmas

Phie Peeters – 18 December 1991

'And behold a great sign appeared in heaven, a woman shining like the sun and decked with a crown of stars.' So we read in the book of Revelation.

We may apply this exalted language to Mary: shining like the sun and with starlight around her.

In the old litany to Mary she is called 'morning star'. This is the first light at daybreak, the first sign of day after a dark night.

In many places in Europe, and particularly here in Maastricht, she shines in a glittering garment as 'star of the sea', and as such is the refuge for many people who, walking in the darkness, look to her for some light.

Was Mary then a star? Did she shine like one? Were there stars at the birth of her son, filling the heavens? Was there then already gold, frankincense and myrrh? And quite apart from the curiosity of somewhat simple shepherds, was there also interest from the great and powerful of the earth? Did they do homage to this child in the crib, her child? Was she then already seen as the mother of God's Son?

You could pick up recent studies about Mary and look for an answer there. You could also make an exegetical analysis of texts which have been written about her and arrive at an answer. But I haven't done any of that. It came out rather differently. During my holiday in the Black Forest I visited my favourite Tabor Church. Or really, I sat there for a while.

Tabor is a special place, a place of tranquillity and reflection.

It was in that church that I came across a statue of Mary. The

43

statue, set high up on the wall, represents a woman, with hands piously folded but not completely clasped. There is no baby Jesus with her.

The statue is gilded, but that's not disturbing, because the figure is simple and the gold somewhat faded. Perhaps the statue was made in 1930, the year in which the church was built.

In the bookcase at the back of the church there are postcards with pictures of a sixteenth-century Pietà and a group round the cross of the same date.

They are in a separate little chapel.

But no one has made a postcard of the Mary I was looking at. She is simple. She is human. Perhaps rather too human, so that the sculptor has put two little golden angels above her head bearing a crown. Sitting there, I was reminded of icons.

Icons are painted from a quite different perspective, because the saints on icons look at us, rather than our looking at them.

This thought suggested to me that I should not just say what I thought of Mary but above all that I should ask her what she has to say to me, to us. This Mary lacks all apocalyptic beauty: no crown, no status, no scarlet robe, not even any blue.

Her folded hands and her inwardness are all that she has, all that make her Mary.

Evidently that is enough for those who visit the church: the lighted candles bear witness to that.

What has she to say, when I think back to her in Bethlehem? The still fresh, young mother, happy with her baby, her son?

Somewhat carelessly we often put a stuffy Joseph beside her, her husband who, though concerned for mother and child, remains in the shadows, in the background. We all too easily forget that these two people loved each other and were happy about this child.

The young Mary is presented in the Magnificat to Elizabeth where she says, 'The Almighty has done wonderful things by me; holy is his name.'

In my view exegetes are right in putting these words in her mouth. It also means that she was worthy, had the worth to say these words. Perhaps not at that moment. That was still rather difficult for such a young girl. At that time it was impossible for her to sense what the Almighty had done in her, and what her still-unborn child was going to mean for humankind.

Only when that intimation became clear in the faith of Easter and Pentecost, only then should her words take us back to Bethlehem.

It is better for us to follow her from the beginning and understand the beginning that is depicted in the biblical sentence as Mary's message. We understand this saying to be 'Let your word come about in me.' That is her complete surrender to God. Her '*fiat*' sparkles with her youth and at the same time her simple humility: the handmaid of the Lord. That was her answer: surrender, readiness, no slavery but a joyful acceptance of what was to be the way that God would go with her. There power emanates from her; there you can sing, rejoice, write verses or just be happy and quiet, withdrawn.

You can listen easily to the youthful Mary. You recognize something of your own enthusiasm then, when you consciously began your life, let us say also in God's presence, choosing a way which also made you enthusiastic and happy.

Mary, this was your spring!

How did your Magnificat sound in the summer? We know so little, but I think that you were very happy with such a son. But what was going on in him, what lived in him? What grew in him? And then there was that day . . .

In his mother's footsteps he goes the way which God wills of him and anxiety seizes you. Every mother must let go of her child, so that it can go its own way. But the way that Jesus chose was to be a hard, risky way, right across all traditions and accepted views: he was to bring God's message and himself be God's message.

And Mary? Perhaps she might put something in his knapsack for the way. That was all. He didn't want any second set of clothes or sandals, or a roof above his head, or even a stone on which to rest his head.

And in his new life Mary no longer counted.

Disappointment, loss and sorrow, she took it into her heart and pondered on it; God's way, my way.

She continued along this course and followed him, from afar or nearby. She understood his message better and better, and the closer they got to Jerusalem, the more her anxiety grew.

How old was Mary when she stood under his cross? Fifty, perhaps?

And even after that she went on, with others, strengthening one another in faith.

And then come the rumours: he's alive! The rumours take on fixed form, there are witnesses. And silently there grows a need, silently the Spirit takes possession of Jesus' followers, the Spirit again takes possession of Mary. This is what we call Pentecost.

For the young church this experience was a breakthrough in faith, to courage and trust, and for Mary light that gave insight, warmth that soothed the painful experiences in her life, a fire which finally kindled anew her love and trust in God, which had always been great.

And so stars come into heaven, lights which illuminate and clarify, which make bright. The insight of the Spirit grows, grows and burns, and in this Spirit we go back to Bethlehem. And there we see the shepherds. Do they belong there? Certainly, for they are the poor from the Sermon on the Mount. And what about the kings, those wise men? They too belong here, since they too, though eminent, bow down before the mystery that God came near to humankind in Jesus his Son.

And finally the choirs of angels? Yes, they too belong there, for they proclaim good news for then and now: a child is born to us, a son is given to us, God is with us. And little Mary? Small in human eyes and great in God's eyes. God, who has done great things to her; of her we may say: 'And behold, a great sign appeared in heaven, a woman shining like the sun and decked with a crown of stars.'

Mary in My Life

Catharina Halkes

The account of my quest for the meaning of Mary for my faith and life falls into several parts. In the first part (I) I describe my personal experiences, feelings and emotions about the Mary of my youth, the ups and downs in my attitude to her image.

In the second, longer part (II), as a feminist theologian I go to work more studiously, and at a number of points – though not completely – investigate what can be said theologically, ecclesiologically (relating to the doctrine of the church) and in religious terms about Mary, both what has gone wrong in many interpretations and positive possibilities.

In a subsequent short part (III), to end with I again become personal.

Finally (IV), I indicate the background to this article.

I Mary: from the past to today

Poetry

Reflection on the significance which the person of Mary and the diversity of pictures of Mary had in my personal life begins in my youth.

Between nursery days and student days my life was full of names for Mary and pictures of Mary. Not only was Mary given as a third name to the three of us, sisters, but in many rooms in my home there was a picture of Mary, usually with a light or a flower. My mother had a great reverence for the saints, so that at an early stage I made the acquaintance of St Joseph, St Anthony, St Teresa,

St Gerard, whose pictures I can still remember clearly, in every feature.

However, Mary did not dominate our home, for everywhere pictures of Christ (the Sacred Heart) and Mary stood side by side without our feeling any rivalry between them. Mother was always going around with flowers and candles, and both the first rose from the garden, in May, and the last, at the end of October, were given to Mary. In the conservatory there was a chest which served as a kind of altar full of flowers and plants (and daisies picked by us) for the saint of the month: Mary in May and October, the Sacred Heart in June and St Joseph in March.

My tenderest and dearest memories are of the May celebrations in church: Mary enthroned on high between the flowers and the candles, in an aureole of light, the incense and the many hymns, 'Beloved May has come . . . ' Everything was fine as long as I could join in the singing and look at her. At that time I just went through the motions of the rosary, since I was never very good at it . . . I felt caught up in a cloud of tenderness, poetry, love: I loved everyone there and it was all peaceful. So that was 'comfort'[1] . . . and afterwards I had to go out again into the cold of the street. I was also at the Roman Catholic girls' school Maria Virgo, and a member of the congregation of Mary at this school, with blue ribbons: later I worked at two schools, Maria Regina and Maria Assumpta, and it gradually got too much for me. For there was only one model for us, girls and women, that of the lowly and chaste virgin Mary. We were constantly told how we had been assigned a task which was well-pleasing to God, being of service, quiet and in the background, modest and invisible. Already then, in the 1930s and 1940s, this no longer matched our experience, and Mary became a shadow in my life.

Anger and alienation

There was a certain breakthrough in the 1950s. At that time we arrived at the period of the 'new theology', of going back to the sources and of purification, and the ecumenical world came more clearly into view.

Those were enough reasons to have short shrift with all the Roman superstition, but also with deep-rooted religion. Anger at the dogma of the Assumption of Mary which had been promulgated (1950); helplessness and shame at getting agitated about the Mary of Lourdes and Fatima, whose picture at that time was being taken round from city to city. I got further and further removed from the veneration of Mary that was being proclaimed to me.

However, I did not allow the May celebrations to be taken away from me, and I brought my children along. Anyone who is born on the Visitation of Mary[2] and is married at Candelmass[3] does not get detached so easily.

But my distance and alienation from Mary were still strong in those years: we had a panel made for our family with all our patron saints and with the various great saving events on it. Of course Mary was also included. However, we deliberately left her out of our picture of Pentecost, because she wasn't strictly necessary. We're now talking of 1956. Does that shame me? At all events it shames the unbiblical proclamation of Mary and all its consequences.

Biblical clarification

The change came when a Reformed neighbour, a missionary doctor who later became a professor at the Free University, invited me, in an ecumenical context, to come and talk to their church about the veneration of Mary. I was not up to that unaided and began to read new books which thank God had begun to appear round about 1960: by Rahner, Schillebeeckx, Guardini and others.[4] My eyes were finally opened when I discovered the Mary of scripture as the first of the believers of the new covenant. I still recall my joy, my perplexity and my indignation that this Mary had not been handed on to us.

On that basis I gave my lecture to the Reformed community. Subsequently, we members of the editorial board devoted the February number of *Te Elfder Ure* in 1962 to the theme of Mary. When I read through my contribution to this number once again, a number of aspects struck me.

Critical questions

In the first place there is my *indignation and anger* which puts very critical questions 'to the ordinary parish clergy and to the conference fathers preaching *ex professo*'. Why do they so often get stuck in a pious description of an elect virgin, in a glorification which simply makes her less important and more incredible for us? Why do they so often let Mary be explained from the Old Testament and so often make her a kind of new phenomenon, as if it was only then that God's action with human beings began? Why was there practically never a sermon about a Christian humanism, about redeemed human beings in this world, starting from the complete person that Mary was? Why do we find so few of the new views about Mary in preaching? Don't priests themselves study any longer, or do they think that the material is too difficult for the 'laity'?

I was then primarily a critical lay person and was terribly cross at the systematic underestimation of the 'dear believers', as if there were no interested and grown-up people among them.

But in the second place I also already had the beginnings of criticism *as a woman* through my angry question why the preacher put the stress on either Mary's virginity or her motherhood, depending on whether the audience at the conference was unmarried or married, instead of showing quite clearly how Mary was about something completely different: her involvement in the saving work of God which gives a very particular and distinct form and content to her virginity and motherhood. And to cap it all I found that in my parish church at the time the only memorable aspect of the feast of 8 December[5] was the announcement of an evening mass with a rosary before it to encourage the wearing of respectable clothes by women and girls!

New insight

In the face of this I put forward my newly won insights from the Bible and faith with conviction.

1. In the first place I was concerned to understand Mary in her *biblical context*. The contrast between Eve and Mary did not mean

much to me, and I mistrusted the stigmatization of Eve as the seducer. I was much more attracted by a degree of parallelism between Abraham and Mary. Just as the divine voice put Abraham at the head of a new and countless people, God's people of the covenant, so that he began to be called the father of believers in the Old Testament, so Mary is the beginning of the fulfilment of the promise made to Abraham and the beginning of definitive salvation. She is the first of the believers of the new covenant. Throughout the biblical message, the gospel of the incarnation is at the same time fulfilment and new promise. The God of the Bible is always a God who speaks and acts, and Mary is now involved for good in God's saving action.

The stories of the annunciation (the announcement of the birth of Jesus), the visitation (the visit of Mary to her cousin Elizabeth) and the birth of Jesus (Luke 1–2.20) are full of allusions to messianic covenant promises and Old Testament patterns of thought. Mary is clearly the representative of the 'poor of YHWH'[6] who look to their God for everything and expect nothing for themselves, either from human beings in general or from a literal fulfilment of the law. This 'poverty' has nothing to do with material need but everything to do with humility. It relativizes human ability and produces a strong sense of dependence on human beings and being open to God's grace. These 'poor of YHWH' belong to the sacred remnant of Israel, the surviving nucleus of those who are faithful to the covenant with Abraham.

Against this background (and yet others – for example the daughter of Zion, the overshadowing of the ark of the covenant as being filled with God's presence) the words of the annunciation and the Magnificat can be understood and begin to stand out. The provisionality of the time of the promise now begins to turn into the final time of fulfilment.

Or as Congar sees the difference between Old and New Testaments, there is a prophetic line of announcement and an apostolic line of the communication of the gift. Mary is the first to live in the fulfilment of the times for which the prophets longed so ardently.

2. In my lecture I then went into the significance of Christian humanism. In those years I was strongly influenced by the Louvain Dominican J.H.Walgrave. Not only his work, and especially his book *Op menselijke grondslag* ('On a human basis', Bussum 1951) had an influence on me. A series of lectures to the Breda Women's guild which I had invited him to give at the end of the 1950s also made a deep impression on me. I had hesitations about the excessive veneration of a supernatural Mary who dwelt with her child in the clouds and thus lost contact and solidarity with our humanity.

The Lutheran theologian Asmussen said in 1958: 'We say yes to Mary the highly praised mother of God, and no to Marianism.'

For to catch sight of a Christian humanism, human beings after the incarnation of God in Jesus of Nazareth, and to live on that basis, two things are fundamental: God has become completely human specifically so as to give us a picture of humanity which is sound and whole. Christ is the representative of the whole of redeemed humanity; he is the new person. Secondly, Mary is the first to be redeemed, the first believer and the radically redeemed person in whom everything is done through the fullness of grace. So praise to Mary is always essentially praise to the recreative power of God's love and God's spirit. Only through God's grace (*sola gratia*) is Mary what she is, the radically and completely redeemed human person, and we still must become what we are (in the making). So there is equality in principle between Mary and all of us: she is on our side.

The creation of a new earth which found its origin in Christ began in Mary. And in that light the last two dogmas about Mary also seem to me to have become clear and clarified. For in them the church means to confess that in Mary redemption has been radically completed by the all-embracing creative grace of God which puts human beings in a position to say yes and give an answer to the offer of grace.

As our belief in the incarnation and redemption which has actually begun in and through Christ constantly grows more conscious, the image of humanity again has a possibility of soundness and completeness. We live in the tension and at the intersection between the grace of redemption that we have received as sheer gift and the way in which it is actualized and given form from within our humanity and with our own forces, forces which are potentials in us, potentials that ultimately once again we have received.

I would want to call this game of receiving and giving oneself form Christian humanism. Complete autonomy is clearly never an issue here, but one can talk of a given autonomy, a sense of the human possibilities to which a life with and in Christ relates. Here Catholic theology is more 'optimistic' than that of the Reformation. We are not just sinners but also forgiven, and it is there that the humanistic perspective of Mary lies. We take the incarnation seriously up to and including the resurrection and the coming of the Spirit and recognize not only a theology of the cross but also one of consummation, of glory. For the Protestant this glory is still a promise; for us it is already a perspective within which we can work. God has always made a covenant with human beings as partners and put us in a position to work with God. In this way this theology glorifies not only God but also human beings. And it is precisely this faith in the perfecting and glorification of human beings, a faith that we still must achieve but Mary has already achieved, which is still unacceptable to the Reformation, or at least was around 1960, when I wrote this piece. However, in its plea for a sober and above all a more biblical veneration of Mary the Reformation was completely right, and I have learned a lot from it.

3. A third point related to the Virgin Mary. I wrote this about it in 1962:

'Our belief in the virgin birth of Christ has only come alive for me now in the sense that in this hour of our history it must become clear that the redemption as a new and final beginning comes purely from God. It is God who achieves salvation and here brings about a radical new beginning of salvation in which the Holy Spirit is the revelation of the creative work of God.

The holy thing that is born of Mary hallows herself (Luke 1.35). This "holy" here does not mean any moral property but is a biblical term from a root which means "separate", i.e. something separated from this world which belongs to God's world. Mary's pregnancy gives meaning to Christian virginity and is for all after her an anticipation of the eschatological reality, an attempt to portray it. So why should one want to force an opposition between marriage and virginity, as if one were of less value than the other, and as if an"ordinary" marriage were not good enough for the birth of Jesus? It is not a question here of being of greater or less value, even in God's eyes. The only thing that had to become clear to us was that at one moment God began the saving work promised from of old and that this beginning started with God.'

Furthermore, virginity in this sense – as being set apart, dedicated and available for the Lord – should be spoken of (and preached) as an aspect and an element in anyone's state of life, as a personal response, namely from human beings to God.

4. And finally I came back to Mary, the *believer*. 'For from what has been said above, in which so heavy an emphasis is put on the initiative from God, the conclusion should follow that nothing much can be said of Mary other than that all this happened in and with her. And then we should be fundamentally failing to do her justice, for the fact remains that she said yes in the freedom of her faith. We need only compare the answer of faith,*"fiat"*, of this simple girl from unknown Nazareth with the enforced silence of the disappointed, unbelieving Zechariah, priest in the religious centre of the capital Jerusalem, at the announcement of the pregnancy of his elderly wife Elizabeth, to recognize the power of Mary's personal faith. She makes herself available for God, through her words, as a daughter of his people. So her faith is a fulfilment of the faith of Abraham, since it is a covenant faith in which she receives the Redeemer but at the same time gives him to the world.

On the other hand, if any faith is a solitary venture, that is even more true of the faith of Mary, since she had to give an answer to a single question (again to be compared with the question to Abraham), and the human reality afterwards brought her no security. On the contrary, Bethlehem, the flight to Egypt, the child teaching in the temple (Luke 2.41–52), Jesus' words,"Woman, what is there between me and you?" (John 2.4), would certainly not immediately have made everything clear to her. But she held out until the outpouring of the Spirit finally showed her link between her personal life, her personal motherhood, and saving history and discipleship. Believing in the Old Testament does not relate to something that is finished but to something that is happening. Those who are called are not given any teaching but recognize that God is at work and is calling them, that they are entering into this action and taking on themselves the tension which the saving event causes in human existence generally. This is the only explanation of Abraham and the prophets. In Mary the people of God was again given the possibility of recognizing that God is acting here and now and that they also have to act in obedience to the call and thus must follow into the unknown. Here believing means making oneself available. A human being has gone before us here to the full, the first of our new time, and she was a woman. She received Jesus in complete availability, cherished him and made him grow, gave birth to him in his incarnation and gave him to the world. However, this attitude is not just peculiar to any woman who becomes a mother, but is the result of a complete human growth of faith. Schillebeeckx points out that redemption is fully human because a woman also plays a role in it. "Mary is the saving translation of this into maternal terms." She is the embodiment of this maternal, caring goodness.

For me the person Mary is an attractive discovery in respect both of what happened to her and also the way in which she entered salvation history. So she should not have been left out of our picture of Pentecost, as a true believer to whom the Spirit came to complete the work of redemption and as a representative of the church of all of us, believers.'

Storm after the silence

That is what I wrote about Mary around 1960. My 'teachers', the new literature which had appeared, had found a receptive pupil in me, and now I at least stood on trustworthy and firm biblical ground which I immediately recognized and could make my own.

From there I could go further, and indeed did so in a chapter about Mary that I wrote in my first book, *Storm after the Silence*.[7] I didn't take any new theological steps in that, but I did ask questions about the way in which various authors, theologians and others, made a link between Mary and 'women'. During these years the first writings, articles and just one book, above all by priest theologians, were appearing on a 'theology of woman' or 'femininity', about woman, nature and vocation, about 'priest and woman', to quote the title of a German book by Ottilie Mosshamer which wholly internalized the usual argument.[8]

This argument, with variations and differences in each author, amounted to the following: Mary is the woman *par excellence*. Only through her can one read and understand the role of the woman in world history. But not only is she the woman, the model for all women; because she brought up Jesus in Nazareth she is also the ideal of any Christian mother.

Therefore, Mosshamer argued, Marian devotion is the best experience for a priest for opening up the metaphysical world of the woman, and important if he wants to get to know women well and to work with them. The recipe is: 'In respect of women, Mary's "*fiat*" means that in the church she cannot lay any claim to rights and is not called to any office but only to service.' Here Mary's '*fiat*' becomes the status symbol of the woman. 'Who else would perform the service of Mary in the church?'

And Gertrud von le Fort[9] speaks of the '*fiat* line' as 'the characteristic, the mystery of the woman. Though this the woman becomes a "help", she stands in the shadow, she goes under the veil. Therefore the veil is the symbol of the woman.'

The great saints of devotion to Mary were men: St Bernard, St Francis of Sales and many others. This doubtless has to do with the experience of celibacy. In the poetry of the veneration of Mary they could lift up their hearts: 'O purest of creatures, O Mother and Virgin'. That first line of a well-known hymn to Mary really sums up everything to which I was then already opposed and which I criticized in my book. Moreover I was glad that there was no separate Vatican II constitution on Mary, but that she was given a sober place and a sober text within the constitution on the church, *Lumen Gentium*. That at any rate is where she belongs. Happily no word was said here about Mary and women, about 'typical femininity', to the limitations and statements of which I was then already opposed.

Feminist orientation

In the ten years which followed I could not get rid of Mary, but I hardly came upon her in my life. I went to study pastoral theology, was appointed to the staff of a centre for training laity in pastoral work, came to the Nijmegen faculty, and became familiar with the Nijmegen student church, but nowhere was any attention paid to Mary, nor was a single lecture on mariology given to the faculty.

Until 1975, when feminism broke through and I experienced something like an earthquake. That then became a new and fruitful stimulus for me once again to tackle the significance of Mary, to deepen my critical questions of 1964 and put them in a proper context. *Storm after the Silence* seemed to be an emancipating book, even a pre-feminist book, but it didn't yet see the connection between the various phenomena. However, in retrospect the title seemed well chosen!

When the new women's movement, feminism, broke through and had its stormy development, one of the first discoveries was that women were becoming aware of their own roots, their own 'selves'. Until then, women had above all been the objects of the dominant culture, to which men gave the tone by their thought and action and determined who women were, what their characteristics were and what did not suit them, and what the relationship between men and women must be. Women had no name of their own, no face of their own in our culture, and above all they did not give a name and significance to the new phenomenon present in the world around them.

All this applied *a fortiori* in the sphere of religion, of Bible, theology, faith and church. Formally this was regarded as the almost exclusive sphere of men, who interpreted the Bible in the light of their experiences of existence and faith, who formulated theology and performed services in the church. Above all God-talk, the images of God, were criticized, but along with them also the predominant images of humanity, especially images of and about women. And of course there was also the question of the significance of Mary in this critical context. She too was portrayed by church fathers, theologians, confessors and council fathers. Now the issue was how feminist theology should outline her image and significance in a way which was neither androcentric nor from a male perspective.

Already in 1977 a group of feminist theologians had the chance to give a series of talks on the radio through the Catholic broadcasting station in the Netherlands. These talks were collected in a book with the evocative title *When Women have a Say*: when women are actively and critically involved with the word, something also happens to that word.[10] In this series Maria de Groot as a Reformed theologian and I as a Catholic theologian made a programme on Mary.

At that time I spoke and wrote about 'another Mary'. I didn't deny the scriptural basis which I had already discovered, but I put the emphasis elsewhere. And so I have remained active, looking critically at theology, at papal writings and popular piety relating to Mary, which is ambivalent but not unimportant. All this resulted in a chapter entitled 'Images of Mary – Images of Women' in 1984,[11] in which old and new lines of thought came together. This marks another phase in the development of the significance of Mary for my life.

Of course there is no question that this is *the* feminist theology about Mary; rather, here was a personal and provisional account of a quest for her meaning, not only for women but also for men, and most of all to remove ambiguity from Christian belief.

II A theological quest for a 'new' Mary

Why Mary?

As a result of the all too easy identification of images of Mary with images of 'woman', many feminist theologians have turned away critically from Mary as being an 'impossible model'. They have really written her off. However, I think that such a reaction is over-hasty. I therefore opt to continue to be concerned with Mary, for the following reasons.

(*a*) Mary calls for *liberation* from the image that men have formed of her and from the projections that a male priestly hierarchy has attached to her. It is out of a deep feeling of solidarity or sistership that I do not want to let her go.

(*b*) It is also necessary for us to *free women* from the still prevalent images of Mary which limit them. So these must be analysed and unmasked.

(*c*) It is also important for the new theological reflections on Mary which are arising that *feminist criticism* and a possible new approach from that perspective should make themselves heard. There are still male theologians who write in an unconcerned way about Mary and 'the feminine' without taking account of the experiences which have been articulated by women themselves.

(*d*) Mary has always been a stumbling block for *ecumenical* dialogue. By virtue of its origin and starting points, feminist theology is primarily ecumenical in purpose and aim. So it needs to take part in this difficult conversation.

(*e*) However, above all I am intrigued by the complex problems which, on closer inspection, also emerge in the study of Mary. I would venture the hypothesis that by the figure of Mary more than any other it is possible to demonstrate how *ambivalent* the church and its theologians have been about human sexuality, and especially about the *sexuality of women*. Models and mechanisms of conversion have finally made Mary an impossible model which is played off against women, which is not critical of men and which has to legitimate the gulf which the church has produced between (feminine) sexuality and the mediation of the holy.

I think it important to formulate these motives. They echo through this contribution, though they cannot be worked out specially here.

Basis in the Bible

We owe the figure of Mary to the Bible, to the Gospels. She has her roots there, but here we must recognize that Mary does not become a clear figure, does not take on a clear form. She is the mother of Jesus of Nazareth, but the evangelists are concerned with the proclamation of Jesus as the Messiah, whose natural mother and brothers are *contrasted with* the family of God (Mark 3.31–35) or are at any rate relativized. Luke counts Mary among those who hear the word of God and keep it, but he also has the saying of Jesus which twists the beatitude on biological motherhood, carrying, bearing and feeding (Luke 11.26–28), in the direction of the value of discipleship. We know that the two infancy narratives in Matthew and Luke were added later out of the need to reflect in faith on the mystery of the incarnation. Especially in Luke these chapters give a vivid account, culminating in two encounters (with the angel and with Elizabeth) and in two key words, '*fiat*' and 'Magnificat'.

Finally, in the Gospel of John a more concrete, historical Mary hardly appears: she appears only in two scenes, one of which, that at the foot of the cross, is increasingly seen as theological symbolism: the mother – the disciple, the *ecclesia* – the church.

So it is good to realize that Mary the mother of Jesus was a historical figure and has her roots in the Bible, but that she has become a symbolic figure in the church's tradition. Mariological thought belongs more to the symbolic themes than to scholastic conceptual thought. Or, to put it another way, the main difference between christology and mariology is methodologically evident: christology is the explicitation of the significance of a historical event, while mariology tries to personify the characteristics of the new humanity in Mary (Pannenberg).

This symbolic element finds expression when, after Justin (*Dialogue with Trypho*, 100.4), Irenaeus seem Mary as the representative of the whole of humanity and introduces the parallel of (disobedient) Eve and (obedient) Mary.

To make things quite clear I want to state emphatically here that I attach no less importance to a symbolic form than to a historical form, certainly when it comes to the deepest layers of the human soul, to which religion belongs. But here there are two different facts, values, revelations. And this statement already leads me to the conclusion that if men want to do justice to the reflections surrounding Mary, virgin, bride and mother, queen of heaven, comforter of the needy, they are right in thinking that theology is not enough: there is also a need to take account of the history and the psychology of religion and of depth psychology.

Degeneration in history

The problem is: how do you look at the history of the veneration of Mary throughout church history? The *magisterium* of the church has solemnly declared Mary *Theotokos* – 'God-bearing' (Ephesus 411), and *Aei parthenos* – 'ever-virgin' (Lateran Synod 649); she is free of original sin (dogma of 1854) and has been taken up into heaven (dogma of 1950). Theologically speaking it must be stated that three of the four dogmas have a christological content and point to the mystery of Christ: the fourth and last expresses the complete redemption of a human being.

So on the one hand a truth of faith about Christ is revealed and established through Mary (i.e. he is truly human and was born of a human mother, his birth is a divine initiative which came about without sexual union, through a woman who *par excellence* was freed from original sin for the sake of the one to be born from her). On the other hand, Mary symbolizes ultimate salvation intended for all people. So Mary never really exists for her own sake but is always a reference to something or someone else.

Hence the question: who is Mary herself?

We already see the split in Ephesus, where Mary takes the place of the goddess Diana or Artemis and gives form to the mystery of the divine mother which is indispensable for human beings. This in fact gives rise to two Marys. First there is the Mary of the doctrine of faith, which always is on guard to see that her person remains subordinate to that of Christ, so that her splendour in no way diminishes or dims the splendour of Christ, and in which Mary owes her excellence to God's grace and Christ's birth.

Secondly, over and above that, Mary lives in a growing and sometimes extravagant piety, not only on the part of 'ordinary people' but also on the part of male saints and theologians like Bernard. This piety has a radiance of its own; it is an evocation which stems from a primal need for what gives, nourishes and preserves life. As long as the gap remains, the confusion will remain, but this heightens the challenge to look deeper.

It is precisely because of the relationship between Christ and Mary at a doctrinal level that feminist theologians (I would mention Kari Børresen in particular) reject the notion that Mary could be an inspiring model for women. Mary represents humanity as the feminine and subordinate partner. A mariology which is based on this serves as a legitimation of traditional sexual attitudes rather than as a source of liberation. The images of bridegroom and bride are one example: in the comparison with God and Israel, or Christ and the church, Mary stands for Israel and for the community, the *ecclesia*; in this typology the feminine identification of the church is in a subordinate relationship to the symbol of the male provider of leadership. Or, to put it another way, the male is the initiative, the leading principle; the female follows but also turns aside; in the Old Testament she is also the unfaithful prostitute.

It is here that the exclusive use of the symbolism of the marriage takes its revenge on a church theology which is orientated on the hierarchy. There is a wealth of images in the Bible to express the relationship of God with his people and of Christ with the community, like the pilgrim people of God, the vine and the branches and many others. Each evokes another image to get nearer to the mystery, but they cannot be reduced to each other, and moreover they relativize each other. Furthermore they simply apply to the dimension of infinity, and one cannot apply them to the changing relationship in society and the church with impunity.

However, all the relational symbols in which Mary is involved – the daughter of God the Father, the mother of the Son, the bride of the Holy Spirit – do not make it easier to discover what is distinctive about the form of Mary. Mary is always used as a relational being, a hyphen being: in other words she is someone who is always connected with someone else as a connecting sign. That is precisely what feminists are now protesting about as they seek to discover themselves and to descend to the roots and the ground of their being. For them Mary cannot be an inspiring figure to identify with as long as she is only there to point (to Christ) and stands in symbolic relationship for the receiver over against the creator.

For example Mary Daly, in *Beyond God the Father*, wants to emphasize the associations of 'goddess' and 'virgin' which have fought free of the grip of the Christian patriarchy for the development of women now, in contrast to the emphasis on the lowly woman which Mary has acquired as a Christian symbol. Here she wants to cut the traditional doctrine of Mary from the 'freewheeling' symbol that Mary also is, the universal goddess who has many names but is only one personality. Such a division does not of course succeed, and ultimately in her next book on Mary, Daly rejects it in the conviction that it ultimately symbolizes a constraint on the goddess and thus a defeat for a society which is more orientated on women.

Fossilization

I fear that if we keep literally to Mary's womanhood and Jesus's manhood, not only will women not be able to get a step further but the church community will not either. Views are still rampant about the womanhood of Mary, her receptiveness and humility, and about the need for the different roles: of the man Christ who was outgoing and the woman Mary who turned inwards. Moreover we see the construction – as W.Beinert rightly observes – of two 'Trinities': Adam – Christ – the male, who point to ministry, with the pope as the ultimate focus; and Eve – Mary – the woman, who are part of the laity.

This way of playing with images is fatal, and I mean that quite literally: such a procedure results in death because it first closes the circle of images and does not allow any new pointers or comparisons within them. It is an idolizing or absolutizing of images which have become stereotypes. Women are bound by

63

them and even controlled by them. The stereotypes make the experience of new symbols which really evoke images impossible. So Christ and Mary are even fossilized into principles and Mary can give no living impulses to make women critical. Views like 'just as the maleness of Christ is essential for his work of salvation, so too the femininity of Mary is essential for the church which is open to this event' (M.Hauke), are therefore misleading.

It can be noted that two people were deeply involved in the mystery of the incarnation – a divine human event: the male person Jesus of Nazareth and the female person Mary of Nazareth. However, the consequence of this is not, nor can it ever be, the fossilization of this life-producing and challenging revelation of God so that it is made of no avail, by arguing from its form that in terms of anthropology and church structures the roles of men and women are now established and sacramentally the woman cannot convey any salvation.

Liberation?

One of the few feminist theologians to have been concerned with the figure of Mary as a theme is Rosemary Radford Ruether. She has worked out the ambiguity of the symbol of Mary, but has then gone on to investigate whether a liberation mariology can emerge.

Since Latin American liberation theology uses the Magnificat as a source of inspiration to make concrete the messianic reality in human and structural relationships, the critical question can be raised as to who uttered this prophetic hymn of liberation and on whose lips this song was put. In his *Marialis Cultus* of 1974, Pope Paul VI mentions this connection very explicitly, but does not draw clear conclusions from it. Ruether points out that a mariology read in the light of the Magnificat can be an important link between feminist and liberation theologies. Here a piece of dynamite is brought into the heavily guarded church building to use on what has hitherto been the traditional image of a saint. 'It is for us who are interested in feminist and liberation theology to set off this piece of dynamite and blast away the outside of the image,' remarks Ruether.

When Mary visits her cousin Elizabeth, she does not go into raptures because she is pregnant but glorifies God's liberating action precisely because she herself is liberated Israel: the lowly who are raised up. In her radical revolutionary words she as it were anticipates the Sermon on the Plain in Luke's Gospel and Jesus' opening sermon in Luke 4. In other words, Jesus' message is meant first of all for all the marginalized who are portrayed in the inconspicuous woman Mary. In her trust and faith in the Messiah Mary is *par excellence* the personification of the church, the messianic Israel, but only if this picture is seen radically and its deepest consquences are noted: in the analysis of power and transformation to service. Just as God has emptied himself for service in Christ and Christ has emptied himself for service for the liberation of his people, so Mary will continue the liberating action of God in the world: the last will become first and those who rule will have to make their way to the kingdom in the ranks of the poor, whose head and model is Mary (as Rosemary Ruether puts it).

Specifically, I would like to put the question here of the significance of the veneration of Mary as it concerns the liberation of a people from oppression, especially in Latin America and in Poland. I think, for example, of the appearance of Mary in Guadelupe, in 1531, ten years after the native population of Mexico and their precious pre-Columbian civilization had been attacked, conquered, defeated and missionized by white Christian Europeans. This Virgin of Guadelupe has become a symbol for the alienated Mexican people which touches their very roots. She appeared on the hill of Tepeyac, the holy place of the Indian virgin mother of the gods, Tonantzin. Music, for the Indians the means of divine communication *par excellence*, accompanied her, and an Indian heard her speaking in his own conquered language. Her request for a temple was in the deepest sense a request for a new way of living, one which touched the innermost depths of the native population. It took two centuries for the church to recognize this virgin Mary and include her in the official liturgy.

However, the church did not succeed in encapsulating this tradition and making it innocuous. The theologian Virgil Elizondo, from whom I have taken this example, puts it like this: 'the advance of Guadelupe (reduced by the powerful to folklore) is the voice of the masses which calls on the elite to leave their economic, social, political and religious thrones . . . ' 'The task of the theologian is not to declare holy or reject the religious symbols of the people but the ongoing relationship of them in relation to the gospel as a whole. In this way it need not be alienating and enslaving but can be saving and liberating, and Our Lady of Guadelupe can for millions of the enslaved be the temple in which and through which Christ's saving presence continues to be incarnated on the soil of the Americas.'

I think that here in this context Mary functions primarily as a symbol and summons for the liberation of the poor population and the rejection of the yoke of alienation, because she is the figure with which a people identify to find their distinctiveness. Consequently, liberation by a female symbol can have a positive influence on the conscientization of women and their struggle against machismo, the dominant male vanity, which is still so present.

And then we also come up against the attitude of the official church and the way in which some bishops or priests use the symbol of Mary and in so doing keep women down. In a number of articles Ineke Bakker has uncovered several points. Over against that there is again the 'church of the people', the people of the base communities who no longer allow themselves to be incapsulated. This is what Sheila Collins writes about them: 'Liberation theology has developed great creativity and inventiveness, as a result of which it is capable of healing and comforting. The power of this is greatest at those points where the symbols of faith become transforming powers for a common political experience. This applies above all to places like Nicaragua, where a fascinating form of popular piety has arisen, a combination of elements of pre-Spanish Indian popular faith, Catholicism, and political proclamation and action. Here the traditionally oppressive symbol of the Virgin Mary is turned upside down by women who have played a great role in the liberation of their country, in turn transforming their religious experience. In the days of preparation for the feast of the Immaculate Conception (8 December) the Virgin Mary is celebrated as a young women, schoolgirl, student, farmworker who was martyred in the fight for the liberation of their land. Mary is then involved in a procession which recalls the fallen heroes and heroines, called on as the one who had helped the people to defeat the Somozists.'

In the meantime it has become clear that veneration of Mary is very complex and has many levels. For example, the Polish Mary is clearly a source of power and inspiration for a people to continue in their struggle for their own identity and independence. But she also has a liberating effect *at least in our eyes* in the experience of faith and the church: and do women derive their own transformation from her?

Letting go or holding on?

At the beginning of these theological reflections I made it clear that I still want to continue my preoccupation with Mary, not least because I do not want to see feminist theology as just a reactive theology which throws away what it doesn't like, out of legitimate anger at and reaction to the bad influence of a misuse of power by the church. Those who want to continue the journey from Israel and the Gospels have to do more than throw things away; they have to make a critical investigation of the roots of history, of language and imagery, and to look at the concrete and constantly changing context in order to analyse what is contingent, what is changeable and what is essential: what is revealing and what must be rejected as a later deposit.

I would claim that the motherhood of Mary was once of fundamental importance, but that it cannot be used to fixate women on motherhood. Specifically in the Gospels we hear in detail the degree to which Jesus relativized physicial motherhood by putting the stress in his preaching on the family of God: hearing the word of God and fulfilling it. So bearing and feeding need not be praised in themselves; it is a matter of following Christ, and if necessary breaking bonds which bind too tightly.

Now the unique thing about Mary is that in her the attitude of 'hearing and doing' coincides with becoming a mother, indeed these were the conditions for that. The unfortunate thing is that her '*fiat*' is interpreted by a male church as a timid and passive reaction to an amazing word of God. But that tells us most about the interpreters. Mary freely and actively says yes as an autonomous person who in believing receptiveness is open to salvation from God and responds to that. If people want to talk about dependence, then they should recognize that here God made himself dependent on a human being, and the human being was receptive to God.

Receptiveness, openness, attentive listening are characteristics of a humane and above all a believing attitude. Allowing yourself to be addressed by another, by what lies around you, by what emerges from the depths of your heart (the whisperings of the Holy Spirit) and acting accordingly; being sensitive enough to be able to distinguish what is important (Phil.1.8–10) – all this represents an attitude which we must not confuse with the passivity imposed on women by a patriarchal society and church. For this is an attitude of the utmost attentiveness and the creativity which flows from it, based on a listening life and on emptying oneself of power and self-sufficiency.

In our culture and church, dominated by human beings and power, this attitude of faith is the primary and necessary task of all males caught up in power and verbal violence. In this connection the theologian G.Tavard remarks that where mariology has gone wrong the cause has been anomaly, the arbitrary juxtaposition of images by male church leaders. If people want to continue to speak in relational images, the *whole* church is a symbol of the listener, the one who is receptive to God, to Christ, to the Spirit. However, people easily forget this when within the church they create levels of speech and silence, of activity rather than passivity, of those in office as opposed to the church people, of a male priesthood as opposed to all women.

The deliberate fixation of sexes in relation to a division of functions and stuctures can only be explained in terms of a notion of power for which any living change is primarily inconvenient and threatening.

From Mary's '*fiat*' (Luke 1.38) now to her 'Magnificat' (Luke 1.46ff.). What always strikes me in particular here is that it was precisely in the encounter of two women, both playing a role in salvation history, each of them pregnant with prophetic life, that the spark of the Spirit flashed over. Mary too was taken out of herself, the child moved in her womb, and all this produced the climate for Mary's prophetic vision.

It is precisely in these situations of creative interpretations of scripture and above all dominant images that I see the task of feminist theology. Our first task is to clear away the rubbish, ask iconoclastic questions and introduce dynamite. Not to blast away the roots of divine revelation or the heart of the liberating message of the gospel, but to blow up the stubborn structures of church and thought which obscure this revelation and thus prevent human beings from making use of its explosive effect. However, this prophetism can only be made fruitful and saving if we 'oscillate' between '*fiat*' and 'Magnificat', in other words if the feminist protest does not become a closed ideology but remains open and accessible to the working of the spirit. Only then can protest turn into prophecy.

If women derive inspiration from the Magnificat, men should meanwhile become aware of the way in which Mary's '*fiat*' is an exemplary attitude for the believer and realize this by really dropping their dictates. The '*fiat*' is not a service of the lofty, who are ready to bow to the poor; it is a matter of entrusting oneself to the inconvenience of the poor, the suffering, those who have been silence and marginalized. It is clear that in the reality of God's revelation there is no longer 'male or female' (Gal.3.28), but a being one in Christ. So we must go along the way, but everyone has much to learn.

Who is Mary for us?

Mary – is she an expression of the feminine features of God?

Mary – is she the feminine face of the church? Mary – is she a female human being, unique through her role in the incarnation of God and therefore first transformed into a prophetess, a trans-

69

lator of God's salvation in realizing what we are all called to: being fulfilled by the divine Spirit, hallowed and divinized?

At the moment I incline to the last possibility, but would immediately add that I still have not solved the problems. However much a liberation mariology helps us a stage further in scriptural terms, it does not bring us to the most intimate levels of the human soul. The remarkable thing is that while the Catholic church certainly makes visible again in Mary the centuries-old 'feminine' element which is oppressed in the patriarchate, at the same time it passes over the content of its revelation and denies the divine element in this feminine which has been experienced by people at all times. This is the root of the ambivalent attitude which dogs and accompanies the ambiguous attitude of the veneration of Mary in all ages.

Moreover it is important for feminist theologians to have a great interest in cultures before the patriarchate in which the goddess symbolizes the primal dimension. In that way they have again discovered, for example, that the church's dogmas of Mary take up the great visions and images of the old religions but drastically change their significance. To give one example: the dogma of Mary's virginity has links with the ancient mystery of the great goddess who was virgin. However, for the goddess, 'virgin' denotes independence, being self-contained, and not the rejection of her own sexuality. The goddess was not dependent for her fertility on a man, and rooted in herself.

In the veneration of Mary, Mary's virginity is originally a symbolic and cultic aspect signifying that she was completely open to the transcendent, completely free for God, intent on God, without any other connection to human beings, *quite apart from any sexual relationship*. However much a fundamental change of meaning already emerges in this last, it will be narrowed down still further to an ascetic *moral* aspect. As a result a permanent stamp is put on veneration of Mary and thus on sexual experience.

Another example is the association of Mary with the moon goddess, the old female image of the ebb and flow of the tide, of growth, fullness and decline, of light and darkness. At a very early stage the division into four times seven days of the lunar cycle was connected with a woman's monthly cycle. It was regarded as the ongoing renewal of life and death, as the primal unity of birth and death, as the origin of all life and fertility. Nor is it surprising that in veneration of Mary at all times married women have prayed to Mary for fertility and that she is experienced as a powerful intercessor 'in the hour of our death'.

In connection with a better insight into the significance of age-old images and myths, knowledge is also needed from psychology of religion and depth psychology if we are really to understand the longings and needs that people carry around in their unconscious. Everything indicates that Western men and women in particular are in search of the lost or repressed soul, the *anima*, which integrates the transcendent dimension in our existence. As long as theology and mariology stigmatize feminine corporeality, eroticism and sexuality as a threat and a snare for human beings, the feminine will be experienced as disquieting and rationalized as dangerous and misleading.

Precisely in a fundamental deepening of mariology in which we dare to believe that God expresses himself in 'primal scenes' (Drewermann), we could throw up a dam against the violence and destruction of a 'father-world', in which power, achievement and rattionality are central and thus one-sided, and as a result have the distorting effect of robbing religion of a deep and important aspect. Only when the church dares to consider all the aspects of the great mother can women be given their due and can a healthy and healed mariology be effective for both women and men.

Marina Warner, *Alone of All Her Sex*, is an important historical study of the diversity of images of Mary connected with images of women over the centuries. In it we can distinguish by means of five of the most prominent images (virgin – queen – bride – mother – intercessor) the constantly changing emphases and projections on the figure of Mary, depending on the way in which the economic, social and church-political situation colours these images.

A study by Eugen Drewermann has given me an even more important insight into the whole problem because it is more fundamental. He unmasks the inconsistency of the Catholic *magis-*

terium when it declares that the doctrine of faith is based only on Bible and tradition and at the same time tries to defend and explain marian dogmas. In this respect we cannot go only by the Bible or by the tradition of the first three centuries. Hence the opposition of Protestant theology, which is offended by a number of elements from mariology as relics from a 'pagan' culture around the Mediterranean. Hence, too, the mistrust of so many people outside the church of the great exaltation of the figure of Mary in heaven and the oppression of women in the earthly church.

It is precisely through the significance of Mary for faith that the church should be able to bring its self-understanding to deeper levels.

Drewermann then mentions four aspects which are important:
1. At the foundations of theological truth, what constantly appears everywhere and sometimes in 'pagan' religions needs to be taken into account. So the author goes further than Vincent of Lérins, who produced the formula that what all believers have believed at all times and in all places in the church should be regarded as Catholic truth. Drewermann thinks that this formula is too limited and not in accord, for example, with the reality surrounding the dogmas of Mary. He argues that the Catholic church should formulate as a principle of faith that what people of all times and places have believed and what they constantly hold and have held to be true in the history of religion independently of each has an intrinsic claim to divine truth. Or, to put it yet another way, as the foundation of a Catholic anthropology: it is unthinkable that God created human beings in such a way that certain religious content should constantly emerge in human consciousness as being evident without being true. The God of creation is no malicious god or evil demiurge. In terms of the history of religion, the mother of God as the origin of all life is one of the earliest religious views of humanity.
2. The rooting of the religious symbols of the faith lies more in the archetypal images of the unconscious than in the categories of undertanding and in the appeal to the *external* reality of historical facts.
3. The gulf betwen Catholicism and Protestantism is the consequence of the inner conflict within Catholic theology itself, because

this last has incorporated pagan elements in its doctrine without being able to develop an adequate theology which dares to be open to the witness of the history of religion and of the deepest levels of the human psyche, instead of disputing this polemically.

4. The dogmas of the Catholic church are to be understood as a kind of *lingua franca* (common tongue) which illuminates the elements of truth in all religions and the recognition of the truth of the human heart, at least as far as the most essential images of its hope and its longing are concerned.

Moreover Drewermann speaks of the return of what was suppressed when in the fourth century the church modelled the image of Mary on that of the Egyptian Magna Mater, Isis, with her child (Horus) on her lap. After the aversion of the patriarchal religions of Israel, Greece and Rome to the goddess, here there is an opening of which the church itself is barely aware. However, it trusts understanding and seeks more of a place of revelation than what lives in the deepest and unconscious dimensions of human beings. Moreover the ambivalence is completely evident in the split between Mary and Eve.

In the relationship between Catholicism and Protestantism, the important thing is that Catholicism can tell Protestantism that one does not deepen faith in God but destroys it if one pays no attention to the psychological and thus also to the historical foundations of the faith. Secondly, Protestantism needs to be aware that God did not create the world with its wealth of images and the human soul with its wealth of symbols promptly to be alienated from it again, but to give people the possibility of a longing for knowledge of God which can be effective.

On the other hand, Protestant criticism of the ambivalent attitude of the Catholic church to the veneration of Mary and marian dogma must continue to ask it to clarify its own attitude and make its theology consistent. Only if it has the courage and the trust, albeit very critical, to form a link with what lives in the human soul will it be able fruitfully to build up, purify, and correct in the light of what is specific to Christianity: the indispensability of the covenant and of divine grace for the human person. However, 'human person' may then no longer be seen as the consciousness reflecting on itself (in current psychological language the 'male principle'), since precisely as a result of that the revaluation of nature, of feeling, of the unconscious, of 'the feminine', all fall outside faith.

I am convinced that the feminist critiicsm of the church's mariology can contribute towards the analyses by Drewermann and others being taken seriously, being studied more closely and developed further, towards a development of the discussion about revelation and experience, about nature and grace, and towards patience not to throw overboard so important an image as that of Mary – however ambiguous it may be – and to make new goddesses.

However, this process can only be credible and convincing if the revaluation of the symbol of Mary goes hand in hand with a renewed self-understanding on the part of women: autonomous (though relative), critically creative and with a positive evaluation of feminine corporeality, human sexuality and our emotionality.

III Mary, found again and revalued

After this heavier part, which digs deeper, I shall end as I began, with a personal word. Mary has again become very dear to me. She is not the image of a subjected, dependent woman, but far less is she a goddess. For me, Mary has become the image of the person who in Christianity came closest to the divine by being completely filled with the Holy Spirit. So we too can see our lives and faith as a pendulum between '*fiat*' and 'Magnificat', between receptivity and praise of God, from which prophetic and creative activity emerge.

Mary as virgin and mother. Is that too far from us and is she therefore an impossible model? I believe that here we have to think about attitudes for expressing our humanity and our faith and growing in it:

motherliness, as an attitude which allows other people to live and grow, but which continues to respect each individual's own freedom and responsibility: an attitude of attentive life in relationship, fruitful life, doing;

virginity, as an attitude of being open and available to the divine mystery, to the voice and power of the spirit in us; from this we learn to live from our own centre, our own roots, in independence, and not in a one-sided and alienating dependence. Thus in my view virginity denotes more a human attitude than compulsory abstinence. Virginity in the sense of 'integrity', of the inviolability of one's own body, can be a powerful influence for women to offer resistance to sexual excess and male marginalization and violation. This holds for women in Latin America who often live in a macho context (cf. Pissarek-Hudelist) but equally applies to all women, including those in our Western culture.

Thus, from an attitude of motherliness and virginity, women, but also men, can grow in relationality and mutual dependence and in human autonomy.

And finally, we may believe in the motherly creative work of the Holy Spirit, the living breath of God, which also ensouled Mary, the *ruah*, the storm-wind of Pentecost, which drives us on, gives us new space; which is very vulnerable and again brings movement to what has become fossilized. 'Be reborn from water and the Spirit' is what Jesus says to Nicodemus. These are the symbols of the female womb and the divine communication of love within the Trinity.

Seen in this way, Mary is not a model exclusively for women but a primal image, a symbol of openness to the mystery of our existence and of prophetic power. The Magnificat calls on us to resist the dominant powers, as the Hebrew midwives with great creativity resisted Pharaoh, and the 'crazy mothers' of Argentina constantly opposed the injustice of the dictatorship.

Thus Mary can be an inspiration not only to women but also to men. For the saying of Irenaeus of Lyons applies to all of us: '*Gloria dei homo vivens*' – 'The glory of God consists in human beings coming to life.'

In the book *Dear Mary, Dear Peter*,[12] which contains a number of letters written by different authors to people from the Second Testament, I said this in my letter to Mary: 'After all these necessary detours I can again come closer to you as the biblical Mary, a woman who has lived in history, salvation history. Slowly

I am also coming to have no more need to draw on you as a symbol for new generations of women, and now with feminist traits. You are who you are, and that is enough for me.

We should no longer allow Eve and you to be played off against each other. That has happened for far too long in the tradition. If Eve is the mother of all who live, then you, Mary, are the mother of all who believe. But most deeply, dear Mary, you have become more than a mother, you have become a sister for me, not striking, but faithful, not "interesting" but strong. And you are so dear to me above all for your vulnerable modesty.'

IV Background and literature

This article, written at the request of the Edward Schillebeeckx Foundation, is based on various of my publications on Mary written between 1962 and 1992.

In general it is more like an essay, since I have dispensed here with scholarly apparatus, references or footnotes, and technical theological discussions.

In general it can be said that this contribution has become a reflection on my articles.

Part II is an exception in so far as in it I have used large parts of my chapter on Mary from my book *Seeking What was Lost*.

To give some idea of the literature on which this article is based, I have added a survey of my own publications on Mary.

This is followed by an extensive bibliography of what I have read, studied and worked on about Mary over the years. It includes work by classical authors about Mary, feminist writings and also non-feminist publications.

To end with, I have mentioned three papal documents by Pope Paul VI and Pope John Paul II which appeared in the 1970s and 1980s.

A few brief comments on these Roman documents:

Marialis Cultus offers a few new perspectives on the connection between Mary and 'women', by going into the diversity of women in different societies and cultures which makes it necessary also to make the picutre of Mary more concrete.

Redemptoris Mater goes into this connection only once (no.46o). This encyclical was written in honour of the Marian Year 1987.

By contrast, *Mulieris Dignitatem* puts an extraordinarily heavy emphasis on Mary, while the letter is in fact about the worth and calling of women. However, this letter, too, was written on the occasion of the Marian Year. Although the pope makes some exegetical and other corrections which feminist theology has meanwhile brought to light, the letter puts too one-sided a stress on women as *par excellence* called to see Mary as their image and model and to follow her. Moreover there is a danger that the symbolism surrounding Mary (virgin, bride, mother) is held out to women as the norm by which they must live in order to express this symbolism.

I have great objections to this for the following reasons:

1. This pope is falling back into an old tradition which thought that the picture which the church presented of Mary applied to all women. If he saw Mary as the model of the radical believer she would be able to be a source of inspiration for all believers, regardless of whether they were men or women, in their need to maintain an attitude of receptiveness.

2. Religious language is *par excellence* a pictorial, symbolic language. Images and symbols can give us greater space and so put us in touch with the infinite. However, if they are used to be imposed on people as values and norms, they are used wrongly and become harmful.

Specific people always live in a historical context, and it does not need to be argued that over the course of the centuries, already in our culture, people have changed a great deal and that this change has taken place more quickly than ever in our century. So images must sometimes be dropped because we no longer recognize ourselves in them, or they must be relativized because they no longer prompt recognition in all cultures. Women, for example, have a great variety of experiences, and certainly not just those of virgin, bride and mother.

Images and symbols can be evocative, can speak to us and

summon us, surprise us and give us space; they therefore continue to attract and inspire people, as good poetry also does. But as the pope imposes images of Mary on women, he binds us by particular expectations, norms and values which we no longer recognize as our own, because they force us into a straitjacket that we have discarded. Images are then absolutized and declared valid for ever. This universalistic, idealizing, abstract language of the pope is misleading, and is fatal for the space which truly metaphorical language should produce.

That brings the opposition that I described in Part II full circle. Only in the light of their present attitude of faith and the specific context in which they live can women – and men too – express their devotion to and veneration of the believing and prophetic Mary of Nazareth.

Publications about Mary by Catharina J.M.Halkes

'Maria de gelovige mens', in *Te Elfder Ure*, 9.2, February 1962

'Als de mist optrekt! . . . ', *Schrift* 38, April 1975

'Beeld van Maria – beeld voor de vrouw in de r.k.kerk?', *Vox theologica* 1975/4, 45 no.4

'Een "andere" Maria . . . ', in Halkes and Buddingh (eds.), *Als vrouwen aan het Woord komen – Aspecten van de feministische theologie*, Kampen 1977

'Drieluik voor Maria', in Catharine Halkes, *Met Mirjam is het begonnen*, Kampen 1980

'Mary and Women', in *Mary in the Churches*, Concilium 168, 1983, 65–73

'Mariabeelden – Vrouwbeelden', in Catharina Halkes, *Zoekend naar wat verloren ging*, Ten Have, Baarn 1984

'Maria – inspirierendes oder abschreckendes Vorbild für Frauen?', in E.Moltmann-Wendel, H.Küng and J.Moltmann (eds.), *Was geht uns Maria an?*, Gütersloh 1988

'An Maria', in *Liebe Maria, lieber Petrus!*, Gütersloh 1987

'Maria', in E.Göszmann et al. (ed.), *Wörterbuch der feministische Theologie*, Gütersloh 1991

Bibliography

G.Ashe, *The Virgin*, London 1976

H.Asmussen, *Maria, die Mutter Gottes*, Stuttgart 1960

I.Bakker, 'Dezoetelijke Maria van de bisschoppen en de inmenging van de paus – spanning tussen kerkleiding en regering in Nicaragua', *De Bazuin* 66.7, 18 February 1983

W.Beinert, *Zal ook dit geslacht haar zalig prijzen?*, Tielt and Amsterdam 1975

————, 'Maria und die Frauenfrage', *Stimmen der Zeit* 108, 1983, 1, 31–45

————, *Maria in der Feministischen Theologie*, Kevelaer 1988

————, *Unsere Liebe Frau und die Frauen*, Freiburg, Basel and Vienna 1989

L.Boff, *Ave Maria. Das Weibliche und der Heilige Geist*, Düsseldorf 1982

K.Børresen, 'Männlich-Weiblich: Eine Theologiekritik', *Una Sancta* 35.4, 1980, 325–34

R.Brown, *Crisis Facing the Church*, New York and London 1975, 84–108

————, *Mary in the New Testament*, Philadelphia 1978

S.D.Collins, *A Different Heaven and Earth. A Feminist Perspective on Religion*, Valley Forge 1974

H.Cox, *The Seduction of the Spirit*, New York 1973 (especially ch.7)

M.Daly, *Gyn/ecology. The Meta Ethics of Radical Feminism*, Boston 1978

————, *Beyond God the Father. Toward a Philosophy of Women's Liberation*, Boston 1973 and London 1985

G.Daneels, ' "Marialis Cultus". Een Romeins document over de Mariaverering na Vatikaan II', *Collationes* 1974, 2, 257–78

H.Dresen-Coenders, 'Moeder, beeld en werkelijkheid', *Dux* 31, 1964, April/May

————, 'Machtige grootmoeder, duivelse heks', *Jeugd en Samenleving* 5, 1975, March/April

E.Drewermann, 'Die Frage nach Maria im religionswissenschaftlichen Horizont', *Zeitschrift für Missions und Religionswissenschaft* 66.2, 1982, 96–117

V.Elizondo, 'Mary and the Poor: A New Model of Evangelizing', *Mary in the Churches, Concilium* 168, 1983, 59–65

J.Feiner and L.Vischer, *Nieuwe woorden over God, wereld en kerk*, Hilversum 1975

E.Gössmann and Dieter Bauer, *Maria für alle Frauen oder über alle Frauen?*, Freiburg, Basel and Vienna 1989

A.Greeley, *The Mary Myth*, New York 1977

M.Hauke, *Die Problematik um das Frauenpriestertum vor dem Hintergrund der Schöpfungs- und Erlösungsordnung*, Paderborn 1982

F.Heiler, *Die Frau in den Religionen der Menschheit*, Berlin 1977

W.Paul Jones, 'Mary and Christology: A Protestant View', *The Ecumenist* 16.6, September/October 1978, 81–5

M.Kassel, 'Maria. Urbild des Weiblichen im Christentum?', in E.Moltmann-Wendel, H.Küng and J.Moltmann (ed.), *Was geht uns Maria an?*, Gütersloh 1988

J.van Kilsdonk, 'De lege schoot', in *Als je zon je vraagt*, Bilthoven 1974, 43–8

R.Laurentin, 'Foi et mythe en théologie mariale', *Nouvelle Revue Théologique* 3, 1967, 281–307

————, 'Marie et l'anthropologie chrétienne de la femme', *Nouvelle Revue Théologique* 5, 1967, 485–515

R.Mahony, 'Die Mutter Jesu im Neuen Testament', in Dautzenberg, Gerhard et al., *Die Frau im Urchristentum*, Freiburg 1983, 92–116

H.Manders, 'Moeder van God, wie ben je?', in Ad Blijlevens et al., *Volksreligiositeit, uitnodiging en uitdaging*, no place or date, 147–57

'Maria in den Kirchen', in E.Moltmann-Wendel, H.Küng and J.Moltmann (ed.), *Was geht uns Maria an?*, Gütersloh 1988

H.Mühlen, 'New Directions in Mariology', *Theology Digest* 24, 1976, 286–93

A.Müller, *Glaubensrede über die Mutter Jesu*, Mainz 1980

S.Napiòrkowski, 'Hoe staat het met de Mariologie?', *Concilium* 3, 1967, 9

C.Ochs, *Behind the Sex of God*, Boston 1977

W.Pannenberg, *Jesus – God and Man*, Philadelphia and London 1968

H.Pissarek-Hudelist, 'Thesen zur Befreiungsmariologie. Möglichkeiten und Grenzen', in Gössmann and Bauer (eds.), *Maria für alle Frauen oder über alle Frauen?*, Freiburg, Basel and Vienna 1989

M.Révész-Alexander, *Eva-Maria-Venus, symbolen van het vrouwelijk wezen*, The Hague 1968

R.Ruether, 'Mistress of Heaven: The Meaning of Mariology', in *New Woman, New Earth*, New York 1975, 35–62

———, *Mary. The Feminine Face of the Church*, Philadelphia 1977 and London

———, *Sexism and God-Talk*, Boston and London 1983

———, *To Change the World*, London and New York 1981

W.Schöpsdau (ed.), *Mariologie und Feminismus*, Göttingen 1985

P.Schmidt, *Maria, Modell der neuen Frau*, Kevelaer 1975

D.Sölle, *Sympathie*, Baarn 1979, passage on Mary: 'Maria is een sympathisante', 47–53

G.Tavard, *Women in Christian Tradition*, London 1973

J.Tiele, *Madonna mia. Maria und die Männer*, Stuttgart 1990

A.Belford Ulanov, 'The Feminine and the World of CPE', *The Journal of Pastoral Care* 29, 1975, 1, 11–23

M.-T.Wacker, 'Die Göttin kehrt zuruck', in id (ed.), *Der Gott der Männer und die Frauen*, Düsseldorf 1987

M.Warner, *Alone of All Her Sex – The Myth and Cult of the Virgin Mary*, London 1976

P.Washbourn, 'Differentiation and Difference. Reflections on the Ethical Implications of Women's Religion', in Judith Plaskow Goldenberg (ed.), *Women and Religion* 1972

B.Waterkott, 'Wenn eine Frau das Lied der Befreiung singt', *Publik-Forum*, 15 May 1981

Roman documents

Marialis Cultus, Apostolic Adhortation of Pope Paul VI

Redemptoris Mater. On the Blessed Virgin Mary in the Life of the Pilgrim Church – Encyclical of Pope John Paul II

Mulieris Dignitiatem – Apostolic Letter of Pope John Paul II on the Dignity and Vocation of Women

Notes

Introduction

1. E.Schillebeeckx, *Het Tweede Vaticaans Concilie I*, Tielt 1964, 19–20.
2. E.Schillebeeckx, *Een democratische kerk*, Utrecht 1989, 5.
3. E.Schillebeeckx, *Het Tweede Vaticaans Concilie II*, Tielt 1966, 59.
4. In his article, Schillebeeckx goes into two views about Mary at the time of Vatican II.
5. H.Häring, 'Met mensen op weg, voor mensen op weg. Over het theologisch denken van Edward Schillebeeckx', in *Mensen maken de kerk. Verslag van het symposion rond de 75e verjaardag van Edward Schillebeeckx*, ed. H.te Haar, Baarn and Nijmegen 1989, 27.
6. E.Schillebeeckx, *God is New Each Moment*, ed. H.Oosterhuis and P.Hoogeveen, Edinburgh 1983, 121f.
7. T.Schoof, ' " . . . een bijna koortsachtige aandrang", Schillebeeckx 25 jaar theoloog in Nijmegen', in *Meedenken met Edward Schillebeeckx*, ed. H.Häring et al., Baarn 1983, 21.
8. Schillebeeckx, *God is New Each Moment*, 123f.
9. Häring, *Meedenken met Edward Schillebeeckx* (n.7), 27.
10. Ibid., 36.
11. Her best-known work from this time is *Storm na de stilte. De plaats van de vrouw in de kerk*, Utrecht 1964.
12. A.van Heijst, Preface in *Zij waait waarheen zij wil. Opstellen over de Geest aangeboden aan Catharina J.M.Halkes*, ed.R.Bons-Storm et al., 78.
13. C.Halkes, *Met Mirjam is het begonnen. Opstandige vrouwen op zoek naar hun geloof*, Kampen 1980, 8.
14. C.Halkes, *Zoekend naar wat verloren ging. Enkele aanzetten voor een feministische theologie*, Baarn 1984, 14.
15. She herself also indicates that in her article, through her thought about Mary.
16. van Heijst, 'Preface' (n.12), 7.
17. C.Halkes, *Met Mirjam* (n.13).

18. A.Brants, 'Maria in de katholieke dogmatiek', in *Tenminste* 1 (*Jaarboek, Voor informatie en gesprek over de verhouding Reformatie/Rome*), Kampen 1980, 29.
19. Brants, 'Maria' (n.18), 34.
20. W.Logister, 'Tendensen in de Mariologie sinds 1950', *Kosmos en Oecumene* 24, 1990, 3, 62.
21. Brants, 'Maria' (n.18), 33.
22. Brants, 'Maria' (n.18), 31–3.
23. W.Logister, 'Tendensen' (n.20), 64.
24. Ibid., 67.
25. C.Halkes. 'Introductory preface' in R.Radford Ruether, *Maria, het vrouwelijke gezicht van de kerk*, Baarn 1979, 8.
26. W.Logister, 'Tendensen', 64.
27. M.Warner, *Alone of All Her Sex*, London and New York 1976, 17.
28. B.Morel, 'Maria, een vrouw om mee te praten', *Kosmos en Oecumene* 24, 1990, 3, 72.
29. Halkes, 'Introductory preface' (n.25), 9.
30. G. van Deuren, 'Maria heeft vele gezichten', in *De Bazuin* 27, 1991, 29, 112–13; E.Maeckelberghe, ' "Nu wij onze eigen weg gaan." Maria in de feministisch-theologische discussies', *Kosmos en Oecumene* 24, 1990, 3, 77.

Mariology: Yesterday, Today, Tomorrow

1. *Jesus*, London and New York 1979; *Christ*, London and New York 1980: *The Church*, London and New York 1990.
2. A technical term for redemption as brought by Christ.
3. At the time the current jargon within the church for what we moderns would call a preliminary draft, produced by a small committee, to be presented for the discussion of all participants.
4. G.Alberigo and F.Magistretti, *Constitutionis Dogmaticae LUMEN GENTIUM Synopsis Historica*, Bologna 1975, ch.8, 251–93, 490–4, 558–66. Also G.Besutti, 'Nota di cronica sul concilio Vaticano II e lo schema "de B.M.Virgine" ', *Marianum* 26, 1964, 1–42; O.Semmelroth, in *Lexikon für Kirche und Theologie. Das zweite Vatikanische Konzil* I, 325–47; G.Philips, in *L'Eglise et son mystère au IIᵉ Concile du Vatican*, 2, Paris 1968, 206–86; G.C.Berkouwer, *Vaticaans concilie en nieuwe theologie*, Kampen 1964, 273–315.
5. Vatican II, which refused to declare Mary 'mother of the church', nevertheless speaks twice about Mary 'who is called the mother of the church' (*Lumen Gentium* I.6; VIII.63).
6. PL 17, 876 CD.
7. J.B.Pitra OSB, *Spicilegium Solesmense (complectens S.Patrum scriptorumque*

ecclesiasticorum anecdota, etc), four vols., Paris 1855, Vol.3, cols. 130–1. The emphasis lies on 'mother church'. Mary is simply *antonomastice*, by transference, called 'the mother of the church'.

8. *Sermo 25 de verbis Evang. Mt. XII 41–50*, PL 46, 938.

9. Rievaulx, *Sermones ex tempore, XX, in nativitate BMV: 'mater redemptionis nostrae'* (PL 195, 223). Textual criticism also justifies another reading of this text, *'mater redemptoris nostri'*. There is no critical tradition.

10. I would refer simply to *Mary in the New Testament. An Ecumenical Investigation*, ed R.E.Brown, K.P.Donfried, J.A.Donfried, J.A.Fitzmyer and J.Reumann, New York and London 1979; R.Brown, *The Birth of the Messiah*, New York and London 1966; J.Fitzmyer, 'The Virginal Conception of Jesus in the New Testament', *Theological Studies* 34, 1973, 541–75; T.Schreider, *Was wir glauben. Eine Auslegung des apostolichen Glaubensbekenntnisses*, Düsseldorf 1985; Marie-Louise Gubler, *Der Name der Jungfrau war Maria*, Mainz 1989; D.Dormeyer, 'Die Familie Jesu und der Sohn der Maria im Markusevangelium', in H.Frankenmölle and K.Kertelge, *Vom Urchristentum zu Jesus*, Freiburg 1987; S.Ben-Chorim, *Mutter Mirjam. Maria in jüdischer Sicht*, Munich (1971) 1982; H.Räisänen, *Die Mutter Gottes im Neuen Testament*, Helsinki 1969; C.Perrot, *Jésus et l'histoire*, Paris 1980, and *Les deux premiers chapitres de Matthieu et Luc*, Paris 1978; Agnès Gueuruet, *Luc 1–2. Analyse Sémiotique* (Mémoire de Diplome, defended in October 1980 at the Ecole Pratique des Hautes Etudes à la Sorbonne, in manuscript).

Recent general literature: W.Beinert and H.Petri, *Handbuch der Marienkunde*, Regensburg 1984, and *Heute von Maria reden? Kleine Einführung in die Mariologie*, Freiburg 1973, and finally *Unsere Liebe Frau und die Frauen*, Freiburg 1989; L.Schottroff and W.Stegemann, *Jesus von Nazareth. Hoffnung der Armen*, Stuttgart 1981; D.Sölle, 'Mariologie', *Handbuch der Dogmengeschichte* 3.4, Freiburg im Breisgau 1978; I.de la Potterie, *Maria in het mysterie van het verbond*, Bruges and Zeist 1990: this book finds the later church doctrines of Mary's vow of virginity, the immaculate conception and virginity 'before' and 'in birth' all too readily in the New Testament texts themselves.

During this mariological congress Heinrich Stirnimann OP, who was present at the congress, gave me his new book which I did not know: *Marjam. Marienrede an einer Wende*, Fribourg 1989.

11. *Mary*, xiv.

12. Ibid.

13. *'Non intendimus gloriosam virginem nostris mendaciis adornare'* (*Mariale super Missus est, Proemium*; see Hilda Graef, *Mary. A History of Doctrine and Devotion* (2 vols), London 1963, I, 270–3.

14. *Ep.*174, 2, PL 183, 353.

15. In III Sent d.3 p.1 a.1 q.2 ad 3.
16. '*Nec existimo huiusmodi frivola ese praedicanda, ubi tanta suppetit copia praedicandi ea quae sunt certissimae veritatis*' (Thomas, *Declaratio sex questionum ad lectorem Bisuntinum*, *Opuscula* XXIV, ed. Mandonnet 3, *Opera genuina theologia*, 247). See also Cajetan's commentary on Thomas, *In Summam Theologiae* III, 1., a. 10 ad 1.
17. J.Moltmann, 'Can There Be an Ecumenical Mariology?', *Concilium* 168, 1983, xii-xv.
18. *Lumen Gentium*, 8, 67.
19. *Mary*, 109–28.
20. The Council of Nicaea, the first general council in 325, held because of the so-called Arian dispute. This was about Arius's view that Jesus was not really divine because the Son was not eternal. It was established that both the Father and the Son are of the same substance, which again led to new confusions; the Council of Chalcedon took place in 451 – in it the nature of Christ had a central place: the council concluded that Christ is truly man and truly God.
21. *Mary*, 91–110.
22. *Mary*, 94.
23. *Mary*, 110.
24. Ibid.
25. E.Drewermann, *Kleriker; Psychogramm eines Ideals*, Olten ⁴1989.
26. *Mary*, 110.
27. *Mary*, 115.
28. Moltmann, 'Ecumenical Mariology?' (n.17), xiii.
29. *Mary*, 115.
30. *Mary*, 132.
31. Alberigo and Magistretti, *Lumen Gentium* (n.2), 564.
32. Published in *Acta Apostolicae Sedis* 66, 1974, 13–18.
33. *Acta Apostolicae Sedis* 79, 1987, 361–433.
34. See E.De Strijcker, *La forme la plus ancienne du Protoevangile de Jacques. Recherches sur le Papyrus Bodmer V*, Coll.Subsid.Hagiogr., Brussels 1961.
35. Christian books which were not counted among the books of the Bible recognized by the church.
36. Docetism is a doctrine always rejected by the church according to which Christ simply seemed to be human.
37. Gnostic comes from Greek *gnosis*, which means knowledge. Gnosticism is a collective name for philosophical trends in which knowledge was assigned a central place in the event of redemption.
38. Pneuma means 'spirit'. This approach seeks to take both the Spirit and Jesus Christ as normative.

39. The Greek translation of the Hebrew Bible, dating from the third century BC.
40. The Latin translation of the Bible from the fourth century AD.
41. Leonardo Boff, *Ave Maria. Das Weibliche und der Geist*, Düsseldorf 1982; *The Maternal Face of God*, London and New York 1987; *The Trinity and Society*, Tunbridge Wells and New York 1988.
42. A technical term to indicate the real way in which humanity is united by Christ with the second person of the Holy Trinity, here applied by Boff to Mary and the Holy Spirit.
43. See e.g. L.Schottroff, 'Das Magnificat und die älteste Tradition von Jesus von Nazareth', *Evangelische Theologie* 38, 1978, 298–313; L.Schottroff and W.Stegemann (eds.), *Gott der kleinen Leute. Sozialgeschichtliche Bibelauslegung* (two vols.), Munich 1979, and *Traditionen der Befreiung* (two vols.), Munich 1980; R.Schnackenburg, 'Das Magnificat. Seine Spiritualität und Theologie', *Geistliches Leben* 38, 1965, 344–51; R.Brown, *The Birth of the Messiah*, 350–65. For a while (above all in the time of Modernism), exegetes discussed whether this hymn was originally an Elizabeth hymn or a Mary hymn (just as the prologue to the Gospel of John was in all probability a hymn from the circle of followers of John the Baptist); see a summary of this dispute in S.Benko, 'The Magnificat. History of the Controversy', *Journal of Biblical Literature* 86, 1967, 26–75, and the standard biblical commentaries.

   At present exegetes are largely agreed that the two traditions (Zechariah/Elizabeth and Mary/Joseph) were originally independent of each other.

Mary in My Life

1. The sociology of religion distinguishes two important functions of religion, comfort and challenge; comfort is the provision of security and refuge; challenge issues a summons, calls for opposition to injustice.
2. The Visitation: the visit of Mary to her cousin Elizabeth. The festival was originally 2 June and is now 31 May.
3. Commemoration of the presentation of the child Jesus in the temple, 2 February.
4. E.g. K.Rahner, *Mary, The Mother of the Lord*, London 1974; E.Schillebeeckx, *Mother of the Redemption*, London 1964.
5. The Immaculate Conception of Mary, dogma 1854.
6. YHWH is the Israelite name of God on the basis of the text Ex.3.14; Yahweh is a vocalization of YHWH, the name which is not to be spoken.
7. Tine Govaart-Halkes, 'Fiat als status symbool Maria de gelovige mens', in *Storm na de stilte*, Utrecht 1964, 186–200.

8. Ottilie Mosshamer, *Priester und Frau*, Helmond 1960.
9. Gertrud von le Fort, *Die ewige Frau*, Munich 1934.
10. Catharina Halkes and Daan Buddingh (ed.), *Als vrouwen aan het Woord komen*, Kampen 1977.
11. In *Zoekend naar wat verloren ging. Enkele aanzetten voor een feministische theologie*, Baarn 1984, 92–100.
12. Raul Neumann (ed.), *Liebe Maria, Lieber Petrus*, Gütersloh 1987.